C-4916 CAREER EXAMINATION SERIES

This is your
PASSBOOK for...

Offender Rehabilitation Aide

Test Preparation Study Guide
Questions & Answers

COPYRIGHT NOTICE

This book is SOLELY intended for, is sold ONLY to, and its use is RESTRICTED to individual, bona fide applicants or candidates who qualify by virtue of having seriously filed applications for appropriate license, certificate, professional and/or promotional advancement, higher school matriculation, scholarship, or other legitimate requirements of education and/or governmental authorities.

This book is NOT intended for use, class instruction, tutoring, training, duplication, copying, reprinting, excerption, or adaptation, etc., by:

1) Other publishers
2) Proprietors and/or Instructors of "Coaching" and/or Preparatory Courses
3) Personnel and/or Training Divisions of commercial, industrial, and governmental organizations
4) Schools, colleges, or universities and/or their departments and staffs, including teachers and other personnel
5) Testing Agencies or Bureaus
6) Study groups which seek by the purchase of a single volume to copy and/or duplicate and/or adapt this material for use by the group as a whole without having purchased individual volumes for each of the members of the group
7) Et al.

Such persons would be in violation of appropriate Federal and State statutes.

PROVISION OF LICENSING AGREEMENTS – Recognized educational, commercial, industrial, and governmental institutions and organizations, and others legitimately engaged in educational pursuits, including training, testing, and measurement activities, may address request for a licensing agreement to the copyright owners, who will determine whether, and under what conditions, including fees and charges, the materials in this book may be used them. In other words, a licensing facility exists for the legitimate use of the material in this book on other than an individual basis. However, it is asseverated and affirmed here that the material in this book CANNOT be used without the receipt of the express permission of such a licensing agreement from the Publishers. Inquiries re licensing should be addressed to the company, attention rights and permissions department.

All rights reserved, including the right of reproduction in whole or in part, in any form or by any means, electronic or mechanical, including photocopying, recording, or by any information storage and retrieval system, without permission in writing from the Publisher.

Copyright © 2025 by
National Learning Corporation

212 Michael Drive, Syosset, NY 11791
(516) 921-8888 • www.passbooks.com
E-mail: info@passbooks.com

PASSBOOK® SERIES

THE *PASSBOOK® SERIES* has been created to prepare applicants and candidates for the ultimate academic battlefield – the examination room.

At some time in our lives, each and every one of us may be required to take an examination – for validation, matriculation, admission, qualification, registration, certification, or licensure.

Based on the assumption that every applicant or candidate has met the basic formal educational standards, has taken the required number of courses, and read the necessary texts, the *PASSBOOK® SERIES* furnishes the one special preparation which may assure passing with confidence, instead of failing with insecurity. Examination questions – together with answers – are furnished as the basic vehicle for study so that the mysteries of the examination and its compounding difficulties may be eliminated or diminished by a sure method.

This book is meant to help you pass your examination provided that you qualify and are serious in your objective.

The entire field is reviewed through the huge store of content information which is succinctly presented through a provocative and challenging approach – the question-and-answer method.

A climate of success is established by furnishing the correct answers at the end of each test.

You soon learn to recognize types of questions, forms of questions, and patterns of questioning. You may even begin to anticipate expected outcomes.

You perceive that many questions are repeated or adapted so that you can gain acute insights, which may enable you to score many sure points.

You learn how to confront new questions, or types of questions, and to attack them confidently and work out the correct answers.

You note objectives and emphases, and recognize pitfalls and dangers, so that you may make positive educational adjustments.

Moreover, you are kept fully informed in relation to new concepts, methods, practices, and directions in the field.

You discover that you are actually taking the examination all the time: you are preparing for the examination by "taking" an examination, not by reading extraneous and/or supererogatory textbooks.

In short, this PASSBOOK®, used directedly, should be an important factor in helping you to pass your test.

OFFENDER REHABILITATION AIDE

DUTIES
As an Offender Rehabilitation Aide, you would assist the Guidance and Counseling staff in their casework, including interviewing incarcerated individuals; assisting with incarcerated individuals' group sessions; maintaining case files; providing personal assistance to incarcerated individuals for the maintenance of family contacts via telephone and written correspondence; assisting incarcerated individuals with completing complex written forms; and explaining rules and procedures. Performs related work as required.

SCOPE OF THE EXAMINATION
The written test will cover knowledge, skills and abilities in such areas as:

1. **Customer service** - These questions test for knowledge of techniques used to interact with other people, to gather and present information, and to provide assistance, advice, and effective customer service in a courteous and professional manner. Questions will cover such topics as understanding and responding to people with diverse needs, perspectives, personalities, and levels of familiarity with agency operations, as well as acting in a way that both serves the public and reflects well on your agency.
2. **Preparing written material** - These questions test for the ability to present information clearly and accurately, and to organize paragraphs logically and comprehensibly. For some questions, you will be given information in two or three sentences followed by four restatements of the information. You must then choose the best version. For other questions, you will be given paragraphs with their sentences out of order. You must then choose, from four suggestions, the best order for the sentences.
3. **Understanding and interpreting written material** - These questions test for the ability to understand and interpret written material. You will be presented with brief reading passages and will be asked questions about the passages. You should base your answers to the questions only on what is presented in the passages and not on what you may happen to know about the topic.

HOW TO TAKE A TEST

I. YOU MUST PASS AN EXAMINATION

A. WHAT EVERY CANDIDATE SHOULD KNOW

Examination applicants often ask us for help in preparing for the written test. What can I study in advance? What kinds of questions will be asked? How will the test be given? How will the papers be graded?

As an applicant for a civil service examination, you may be wondering about some of these things. Our purpose here is to suggest effective methods of advance study and to describe civil service examinations.

Your chances for success on this examination can be increased if you know how to prepare. Those "pre-examination jitters" can be reduced if you know what to expect. You can even experience an adventure in good citizenship if you know why civil service exams are given.

B. WHY ARE CIVIL SERVICE EXAMINATIONS GIVEN?

Civil service examinations are important to you in two ways. As a citizen, you want public jobs filled by employees who know how to do their work. As a job seeker, you want a fair chance to compete for that job on an equal footing with other candidates. The best-known means of accomplishing this two-fold goal is the competitive examination.

Exams are widely publicized throughout the nation. They may be administered for jobs in federal, state, city, municipal, town or village governments or agencies.

Any citizen may apply, with some limitations, such as the age or residence of applicants. Your experience and education may be reviewed to see whether you meet the requirements for the particular examination. When these requirements exist, they are reasonable and applied consistently to all applicants. Thus, a competitive examination may cause you some uneasiness now, but it is your privilege and safeguard.

C. HOW ARE CIVIL SERVICE EXAMS DEVELOPED?

Examinations are carefully written by trained technicians who are specialists in the field known as "psychological measurement," in consultation with recognized authorities in the field of work that the test will cover. These experts recommend the subject matter areas or skills to be tested; only those knowledges or skills important to your success on the job are included. The most reliable books and source materials available are used as references. Together, the experts and technicians judge the difficulty level of the questions.

Test technicians know how to phrase questions so that the problem is clearly stated. Their ethics do not permit "trick" or "catch" questions. Questions may have been tried out on sample groups, or subjected to statistical analysis, to determine their usefulness.

Written tests are often used in combination with performance tests, ratings of training and experience, and oral interviews. All of these measures combine to form the best-known means of finding the right person for the right job.

II. HOW TO PASS THE WRITTEN TEST

A. NATURE OF THE EXAMINATION

To prepare intelligently for civil service examinations, you should know how they differ from school examinations you have taken. In school you were assigned certain definite pages to read or subjects to cover. The examination questions were quite detailed and usually emphasized memory. Civil service exams, on the other hand, try to discover your present ability to perform the duties of a position, plus your potentiality to learn these duties. In other words, a civil service exam attempts to predict how successful you will be. Questions cover such a broad area that they cannot be as minute and detailed as school exam questions.

In the public service similar kinds of work, or positions, are grouped together in one "class." This process is known as *position-classification*. All the positions in a class are paid according to the salary range for that class. One class title covers all of these positions, and they are all tested by the same examination.

B. FOUR BASIC STEPS

1) Study the announcement

How, then, can you know what subjects to study? Our best answer is: "Learn as much as possible about the class of positions for which you've applied." The exam will test the knowledge, skills and abilities needed to do the work.

Your most valuable source of information about the position you want is the official exam announcement. This announcement lists the training and experience qualifications. Check these standards and apply only if you come reasonably close to meeting them.

The brief description of the position in the examination announcement offers some clues to the subjects which will be tested. Think about the job itself. Review the duties in your mind. Can you perform them, or are there some in which you are rusty? Fill in the blank spots in your preparation.

Many jurisdictions preview the written test in the exam announcement by including a section called "Knowledge and Abilities Required," "Scope of the Examination," or some similar heading. Here you will find out specifically what fields will be tested.

2) Review your own background

Once you learn in general what the position is all about, and what you need to know to do the work, ask yourself which subjects you already know fairly well and which need improvement. You may wonder whether to concentrate on improving your strong areas or on building some background in your fields of weakness. When the announcement has specified "some knowledge" or "considerable knowledge," or has used adjectives like "beginning principles of…" or "advanced … methods," you can get a clue as to the number and difficulty of questions to be asked in any given field. More questions, and hence broader coverage, would be included for those subjects which are more important in the work. Now weigh your strengths and weaknesses against the job requirements and prepare accordingly.

3) Determine the level of the position

Another way to tell how intensively you should prepare is to understand the level of the job for which you are applying. Is it the entering level? In other words, is this the position in which beginners in a field of work are hired? Or is it an intermediate or advanced level? Sometimes this is indicated by such words as "Junior" or "Senior" in the class title. Other jurisdictions use Roman numerals to designate the level – Clerk I, Clerk II, for example. The word "Supervisor" sometimes appears in the title. If the level is not indicated by the title, check the description of duties. Will you be working under very close supervision, or will you have responsibility for independent decisions in this work?

4) Choose appropriate study materials

Now that you know the subjects to be examined and the relative amount of each subject to be covered, you can choose suitable study materials. For beginning level jobs, or even advanced ones, if you have a pronounced weakness in some aspect of your training, read a modern, standard textbook in that field. Be sure it is up to date and has general coverage. Such books are normally available at your library, and the librarian will be glad to help you locate one. For entry-level positions, questions of appropriate difficulty are chosen – neither highly advanced questions, nor those too simple. Such questions require careful thought but not advanced training.

If the position for which you are applying is technical or advanced, you will read more advanced, specialized material. If you are already familiar with the basic principles of your field, elementary textbooks would waste your time. Concentrate on advanced textbooks and technical periodicals. Think through the concepts and review difficult problems in your field.

These are all general sources. You can get more ideas on your own initiative, following these leads. For example, training manuals and publications of the government agency which employs workers in your field can be useful, particularly for technical and professional positions. A letter or visit to the government department involved may result in more specific study suggestions, and certainly will provide you with a more definite idea of the exact nature of the position you are seeking.

III. KINDS OF TESTS

Tests are used for purposes other than measuring knowledge and ability to perform specified duties. For some positions, it is equally important to test ability to make adjustments to new situations or to profit from training. In others, basic mental abilities not dependent on information are essential. Questions which test these things may not appear as pertinent to the duties of the position as those which test for knowledge and information. Yet they are often highly important parts of a fair examination. For very general questions, it is almost impossible to help you direct your study efforts. What we can do is to point out some of the more common of these general abilities needed in public service positions and describe some typical questions.

1) General information

Broad, general information has been found useful for predicting job success in some kinds of work. This is tested in a variety of ways, from vocabulary lists to questions about current events. Basic background in some field of work, such as sociology or economics, may be sampled in a group of questions. Often these are principles which have become familiar to most persons through exposure rather than through formal training. It is difficult to advise you how to study for these questions; being alert to the world around you is our best suggestion.

2) Verbal ability

An example of an ability needed in many positions is verbal or language ability. Verbal ability is, in brief, the ability to use and understand words. Vocabulary and grammar tests are typical measures of this ability. Reading comprehension or paragraph interpretation questions are common in many kinds of civil service tests. You are given a paragraph of written material and asked to find its central meaning.

3) Numerical ability

Number skills can be tested by the familiar arithmetic problem, by checking paired lists of numbers to see which are alike and which are different, or by interpreting charts and graphs. In the latter test, a graph may be printed in the test booklet which you are asked to use as the basis for answering questions.

4) Observation

A popular test for law-enforcement positions is the observation test. A picture is shown to you for several minutes, then taken away. Questions about the picture test your ability to observe both details and larger elements.

5) Following directions

In many positions in the public service, the employee must be able to carry out written instructions dependably and accurately. You may be given a chart with several columns, each column listing a variety of information. The questions require you to carry out directions involving the information given in the chart.

6) Skills and aptitudes

Performance tests effectively measure some manual skills and aptitudes. When the skill is one in which you are trained, such as typing or shorthand, you can practice. These tests are often very much like those given in business school or high school courses. For many of the other skills and aptitudes, however, no short-time preparation can be made. Skills and abilities natural to you or that you have developed throughout your lifetime are being tested.

Many of the general questions just described provide all the data needed to answer the questions and ask you to use your reasoning ability to find the answers. Your best preparation for these tests, as well as for tests of facts and ideas, is to be at your physical and mental best. You, no doubt, have your own methods of getting into an exam-taking mood and keeping "in shape." The next section lists some ideas on this subject.

IV. KINDS OF QUESTIONS

Only rarely is the "essay" question, which you answer in narrative form, used in civil service tests. Civil service tests are usually of the short-answer type. Full instructions for answering these questions will be given to you at the examination. But in case this is your first experience with short-answer questions and separate answer sheets, here is what you need to know:

1) Multiple-choice Questions

Most popular of the short-answer questions is the "multiple choice" or "best answer" question. It can be used, for example, to test for factual knowledge, ability to solve problems or judgment in meeting situations found at work.

A multiple-choice question is normally one of three types—
- It can begin with an incomplete statement followed by several possible endings. You are to find the one ending which *best* completes the statement, although some of the others may not be entirely wrong.
- It can also be a complete statement in the form of a question which is answered by choosing one of the statements listed.

- It can be in the form of a problem – again you select the best answer.

Here is an example of a multiple-choice question with a discussion which should give you some clues as to the method for choosing the right answer:

When an employee has a complaint about his assignment, the action which will *best* help him overcome his difficulty is to
  A. discuss his difficulty with his coworkers
  B. take the problem to the head of the organization
  C. take the problem to the person who gave him the assignment
  D. say nothing to anyone about his complaint

In answering this question, you should study each of the choices to find which is best. Consider choice "A" – Certainly an employee may discuss his complaint with fellow employees, but no change or improvement can result, and the complaint remains unresolved. Choice "B" is a poor choice since the head of the organization probably does not know what assignment you have been given, and taking your problem to him is known as "going over the head" of the supervisor. The supervisor, or person who made the assignment, is the person who can clarify it or correct any injustice. Choice "C" is, therefore, correct. To say nothing, as in choice "D," is unwise. Supervisors have and interest in knowing the problems employees are facing, and the employee is seeking a solution to his problem.

2) True/False Questions

The "true/false" or "right/wrong" form of question is sometimes used. Here a complete statement is given. Your job is to decide whether the statement is right or wrong.

SAMPLE: A roaming cell-phone call to a nearby city costs less than a non-roaming call to a distant city.

This statement is wrong, or false, since roaming calls are more expensive.

This is not a complete list of all possible question forms, although most of the others are variations of these common types. You will always get complete directions for answering questions. Be sure you understand *how* to mark your answers – ask questions until you do.

V. RECORDING YOUR ANSWERS

Computer terminals are used more and more today for many different kinds of exams.

For an examination with very few applicants, you may be told to record your answers in the test booklet itself. Separate answer sheets are much more common. If this separate answer sheet is to be scored by machine – and this is often the case – it is highly important that you mark your answers correctly in order to get credit.

An electronic scoring machine is often used in civil service offices because of the speed with which papers can be scored. Machine-scored answer sheets must be marked with a pencil, which will be given to you. This pencil has a high graphite content which responds to the electronic scoring machine. As a matter of fact, stray dots may register as answers, so do not let your pencil rest on the answer sheet while you are pondering the correct answer. Also, if your pencil lead breaks or is otherwise defective, ask for another.

Since the answer sheet will be dropped in a slot in the scoring machine, be careful not to bend the corners or get the paper crumpled.

The answer sheet normally has five vertical columns of numbers, with 30 numbers to a column. These numbers correspond to the question numbers in your test booklet. After each number, going across the page are four or five pairs of dotted lines. These short dotted lines have small letters or numbers above them. The first two pairs may also have a "T" or "F" above the letters. This indicates that the first two pairs only are to be used if the questions are of the true-false type. If the questions are multiple choice, disregard the "T" and "F" and pay attention only to the small letters or numbers.

Answer your questions in the manner of the sample that follows:

32. The largest city in the United States is
    A. Washington, D.C.
    B. New York City
    C. Chicago
    D. Detroit
    E. San Francisco

1) Choose the answer you think is best. (New York City is the largest, so "B" is correct.)
2) Find the row of dotted lines numbered the same as the question you are answering. (Find row number 32)
3) Find the pair of dotted lines corresponding to the answer. (Find the pair of lines under the mark "B.")
4) Make a solid black mark between the dotted lines.

VI. BEFORE THE TEST

Common sense will help you find procedures to follow to get ready for an examination. Too many of us, however, overlook these sensible measures. Indeed, nervousness and fatigue have been found to be the most serious reasons why applicants fail to do their best on civil service tests. Here is a list of reminders:

- Begin your preparation early – Don't wait until the last minute to go scurrying around for books and materials or to find out what the position is all about.
- Prepare continuously – An hour a night for a week is better than an all-night cram session. This has been definitely established. What is more, a night a week for a month will return better dividends than crowding your study into a shorter period of time.
- Locate the place of the exam – You have been sent a notice telling you when and where to report for the examination. If the location is in a different town or otherwise unfamiliar to you, it would be well to inquire the best route and learn something about the building.
- Relax the night before the test – Allow your mind to rest. Do not study at all that night. Plan some mild recreation or diversion; then go to bed early and get a good night's sleep.
- Get up early enough to make a leisurely trip to the place for the test – This way unforeseen events, traffic snarls, unfamiliar buildings, etc. will not upset you.
- Dress comfortably – A written test is not a fashion show. You will be known by number and not by name, so wear something comfortable.

- Leave excess paraphernalia at home – Shopping bags and odd bundles will get in your way. You need bring only the items mentioned in the official notice you received; usually everything you need is provided. Do not bring reference books to the exam. They will only confuse those last minutes and be taken away from you when in the test room.
- Arrive somewhat ahead of time – If because of transportation schedules you must get there very early, bring a newspaper or magazine to take your mind off yourself while waiting.
- Locate the examination room – When you have found the proper room, you will be directed to the seat or part of the room where you will sit. Sometimes you are given a sheet of instructions to read while you are waiting. Do not fill out any forms until you are told to do so; just read them and be prepared.
- Relax and prepare to listen to the instructions
- If you have any physical problem that may keep you from doing your best, be sure to tell the test administrator. If you are sick or in poor health, you really cannot do your best on the exam. You can come back and take the test some other time.

VII. AT THE TEST

The day of the test is here and you have the test booklet in your hand. The temptation to get going is very strong. Caution! There is more to success than knowing the right answers. You must know how to identify your papers and understand variations in the type of short-answer question used in this particular examination. Follow these suggestions for maximum results from your efforts:

1) Cooperate with the monitor

The test administrator has a duty to create a situation in which you can be as much at ease as possible. He will give instructions, tell you when to begin, check to see that you are marking your answer sheet correctly, and so on. He is not there to guard you, although he will see that your competitors do not take unfair advantage. He wants to help you do your best.

2) Listen to all instructions

Don't jump the gun! Wait until you understand all directions. In most civil service tests you get more time than you need to answer the questions. So don't be in a hurry. Read each word of instructions until you clearly understand the meaning. Study the examples, listen to all announcements and follow directions. Ask questions if you do not understand what to do.

3) Identify your papers

Civil service exams are usually identified by number only. You will be assigned a number; you must not put your name on your test papers. Be sure to copy your number correctly. Since more than one exam may be given, copy your exact examination title.

4) Plan your time

Unless you are told that a test is a "speed" or "rate of work" test, speed itself is usually not important. Time enough to answer all the questions will be provided, but this does not mean that you have all day. An overall time limit has been set. Divide the total time (in minutes) by the number of questions to determine the approximate time you have for each question.

5) Do not linger over difficult questions

If you come across a difficult question, mark it with a paper clip (useful to have along) and come back to it when you have been through the booklet. One caution if you do this – be sure to skip a number on your answer sheet as well. Check often to be sure that you have not lost your place and that you are marking in the row numbered the same as the question you are answering.

6) Read the questions

Be sure you know what the question asks! Many capable people are unsuccessful because they failed to *read* the questions correctly.

7) Answer all questions

Unless you have been instructed that a penalty will be deducted for incorrect answers, it is better to guess than to omit a question.

8) Speed tests

It is often better NOT to guess on speed tests. It has been found that on timed tests people are tempted to spend the last few seconds before time is called in marking answers at random – without even reading them – in the hope of picking up a few extra points. To discourage this practice, the instructions may warn you that your score will be "corrected" for guessing. That is, a penalty will be applied. The incorrect answers will be deducted from the correct ones, or some other penalty formula will be used.

9) Review your answers

If you finish before time is called, go back to the questions you guessed or omitted to give them further thought. Review other answers if you have time.

10) Return your test materials

If you are ready to leave before others have finished or time is called, take ALL your materials to the monitor and leave quietly. Never take any test material with you. The monitor can discover whose papers are not complete, and taking a test booklet may be grounds for disqualification.

VIII. EXAMINATION TECHNIQUES

1) Read the general instructions carefully. These are usually printed on the first page of the exam booklet. As a rule, these instructions refer to the timing of the examination; the fact that you should not start work until the signal and must stop work at a signal, etc. If there are any *special* instructions, such as a choice of questions to be answered, make sure that you note this instruction carefully.

2) When you are ready to start work on the examination, that is as soon as the signal has been given, read the instructions to each question booklet, underline any key words or phrases, such as *least, best, outline, describe* and the like. In this way you will tend to answer as requested rather than discover on reviewing your paper that you *listed without describing*, that you selected the *worst* choice rather than the *best* choice, etc.

3) If the examination is of the objective or multiple-choice type – that is, each question will also give a series of possible answers: A, B, C or D, and you are called upon to select the best answer and write the letter next to that answer on your answer paper – it is advisable to start answering each question in turn. There may be anywhere from 50 to 100 such questions in the three or four hours allotted and you can see how much time would be taken if you read through all the questions before beginning to answer any. Furthermore, if you come across a question or group of questions which you know would be difficult to answer, it would undoubtedly affect your handling of all the other questions.

4) If the examination is of the essay type and contains but a few questions, it is a moot point as to whether you should read all the questions before starting to answer any one. Of course, if you are given a choice – say five out of seven and the like – then it is essential to read all the questions so you can eliminate the two that are most difficult. If, however, you are asked to answer all the questions, there may be danger in trying to answer the easiest one first because you may find that you will spend too much time on it. The best technique is to answer the first question, then proceed to the second, etc.

5) Time your answers. Before the exam begins, write down the time it started, then add the time allowed for the examination and write down the time it must be completed, then divide the time available somewhat as follows:
   - If 3-1/2 hours are allowed, that would be 210 minutes. If you have 80 objective-type questions, that would be an average of 2-1/2 minutes per question. Allow yourself no more than 2 minutes per question, or a total of 160 minutes, which will permit about 50 minutes to review.
   - If for the time allotment of 210 minutes there are 7 essay questions to answer, that would average about 30 minutes a question. Give yourself only 25 minutes per question so that you have about 35 minutes to review.

6) The most important instruction is to *read each question* and make sure you know what is wanted. The second most important instruction is to *time yourself properly* so that you answer every question. The third most important instruction is to *answer every question*. Guess if you have to but include something for each question. Remember that you will receive no credit for a blank and will probably receive some credit if you write something in answer to an essay question. If you guess a letter – say "B" for a multiple-choice question – you may have guessed right. If you leave a blank as an answer to a multiple-choice question, the examiners may respect your feelings but it will not add a point to your score. Some exams may penalize you for wrong answers, so in such cases *only*, you may not want to guess unless you have some basis for your answer.

7) Suggestions
   a. Objective-type questions
      1. Examine the question booklet for proper sequence of pages and questions
      2. Read all instructions carefully
      3. Skip any question which seems too difficult; return to it after all other questions have been answered
      4. Apportion your time properly; do not spend too much time on any single question or group of questions

5. Note and underline key words – *all, most, fewest, least, best, worst, same, opposite*, etc.
6. Pay particular attention to negatives
7. Note unusual option, e.g., unduly long, short, complex, different or similar in content to the body of the question
8. Observe the use of "hedging" words – *probably, may, most likely*, etc.
9. Make sure that your answer is put next to the same number as the question
10. Do not second-guess unless you have good reason to believe the second answer is definitely more correct
11. Cross out original answer if you decide another answer is more accurate; do not erase until you are ready to hand your paper in
12. Answer all questions; guess unless instructed otherwise
13. Leave time for review

b. Essay questions
1. Read each question carefully
2. Determine exactly what is wanted. Underline key words or phrases.
3. Decide on outline or paragraph answer
4. Include many different points and elements unless asked to develop any one or two points or elements
5. Show impartiality by giving pros and cons unless directed to select one side only
6. Make and write down any assumptions you find necessary to answer the questions
7. Watch your English, grammar, punctuation and choice of words
8. Time your answers; don't crowd material

8) Answering the essay question

Most essay questions can be answered by framing the specific response around several key words or ideas. Here are a few such key words or ideas:

M's: manpower, materials, methods, money, management
P's: purpose, program, policy, plan, procedure, practice, problems, pitfalls, personnel, public relations

a. Six basic steps in handling problems:
1. Preliminary plan and background development
2. Collect information, data and facts
3. Analyze and interpret information, data and facts
4. Analyze and develop solutions as well as make recommendations
5. Prepare report and sell recommendations
6. Install recommendations and follow up effectiveness

b. Pitfalls to avoid
1. *Taking things for granted* – A statement of the situation does not necessarily imply that each of the elements is necessarily true; for example, a complaint may be invalid and biased so that all that can be taken for granted is that a complaint has been registered

2. *Considering only one side of a situation* – Wherever possible, indicate several alternatives and then point out the reasons you selected the best one
3. *Failing to indicate follow up* – Whenever your answer indicates action on your part, make certain that you will take proper follow-up action to see how successful your recommendations, procedures or actions turn out to be
4. *Taking too long in answering any single question* – Remember to time your answers properly

IX. AFTER THE TEST

Scoring procedures differ in detail among civil service jurisdictions although the general principles are the same. Whether the papers are hand-scored or graded by machine we have described, they are nearly always graded by number. That is, the person who marks the paper knows only the number – never the name – of the applicant. Not until all the papers have been graded will they be matched with names. If other tests, such as training and experience or oral interview ratings have been given, scores will be combined. Different parts of the examination usually have different weights. For example, the written test might count 60 percent of the final grade, and a rating of training and experience 40 percent. In many jurisdictions, veterans will have a certain number of points added to their grades.

After the final grade has been determined, the names are placed in grade order and an eligible list is established. There are various methods for resolving ties between those who get the same final grade – probably the most common is to place first the name of the person whose application was received first. Job offers are made from the eligible list in the order the names appear on it. You will be notified of your grade and your rank as soon as all these computations have been made. This will be done as rapidly as possible.

People who are found to meet the requirements in the announcement are called "eligibles." Their names are put on a list of eligible candidates. An eligible's chances of getting a job depend on how high he stands on this list and how fast agencies are filling jobs from the list.

When a job is to be filled from a list of eligibles, the agency asks for the names of people on the list of eligibles for that job. When the civil service commission receives this request, it sends to the agency the names of the three people highest on this list. Or, if the job to be filled has specialized requirements, the office sends the agency the names of the top three persons who meet these requirements from the general list.

The appointing officer makes a choice from among the three people whose names were sent to him. If the selected person accepts the appointment, the names of the others are put back on the list to be considered for future openings.

That is the rule in hiring from all kinds of eligible lists, whether they are for typist, carpenter, chemist, or something else. For every vacancy, the appointing officer has his choice of any one of the top three eligibles on the list. This explains why the person whose name is on top of the list sometimes does not get an appointment when some of the persons lower on the list do. If the appointing officer chooses the second or third eligible, the No. 1 eligible does not get a job at once, but stays on the list until he is appointed or the list is terminated.

X. HOW TO PASS THE INTERVIEW TEST

The examination for which you applied requires an oral interview test. You have already taken the written test and you are now being called for the interview test – the final part of the formal examination.

You may think that it is not possible to prepare for an interview test and that there are no procedures to follow during an interview. Our purpose is to point out some things you can do in advance that will help you and some good rules to follow and pitfalls to avoid while you are being interviewed.

What is an interview supposed to test?

The written examination is designed to test the technical knowledge and competence of the candidate; the oral is designed to evaluate intangible qualities, not readily measured otherwise, and to establish a list showing the relative fitness of each candidate – as measured against his competitors – for the position sought. Scoring is not on the basis of "right" and "wrong," but on a sliding scale of values ranging from "not passable" to "outstanding." As a matter of fact, it is possible to achieve a relatively low score without a single "incorrect" answer because of evident weakness in the qualities being measured.

Occasionally, an examination may consist entirely of an oral test – either an individual or a group oral. In such cases, information is sought concerning the technical knowledges and abilities of the candidate, since there has been no written examination for this purpose. More commonly, however, an oral test is used to supplement a written examination.

Who conducts interviews?

The composition of oral boards varies among different jurisdictions. In nearly all, a representative of the personnel department serves as chairman. One of the members of the board may be a representative of the department in which the candidate would work. In some cases, "outside experts" are used, and, frequently, a businessman or some other representative of the general public is asked to serve. Labor and management or other special groups may be represented. The aim is to secure the services of experts in the appropriate field.

However the board is composed, it is a good idea (and not at all improper or unethical) to ascertain in advance of the interview who the members are and what groups they represent. When you are introduced to them, you will have some idea of their backgrounds and interests, and at least you will not stutter and stammer over their names.

What should be done before the interview?

While knowledge about the board members is useful and takes some of the surprise element out of the interview, there is other preparation which is more substantive. It *is* possible to prepare for an oral interview – in several ways:

1) Keep a copy of your application and review it carefully before the interview

This may be the only document before the oral board, and the starting point of the interview. Know what education and experience you have listed there, and the sequence and dates of all of it. Sometimes the board will ask you to review the highlights of your experience for them; you should not have to hem and haw doing it.

2) Study the class specification and the examination announcement

Usually, the oral board has one or both of these to guide them. The qualities, characteristics or knowledges required by the position sought are stated in these documents. They offer valuable clues as to the nature of the oral interview. For example, if the job involves supervisory responsibilities, the announcement will usually indicate that knowledge of modern supervisory methods and the qualifications of the candidate as a supervisor will be tested. If so, you can expect such questions, frequently in the form of a hypothetical situation which you are expected to solve. NEVER go into an oral without knowledge of the duties and responsibilities of the job you seek.

3) Think through each qualification required

Try to visualize the kind of questions you would ask if you were a board member. How well could you answer them? Try especially to appraise your own knowledge and background in each area, *measured against the job sought*, and identify any areas in which you are weak. Be critical and realistic – do not flatter yourself.

4) Do some general reading in areas in which you feel you may be weak

For example, if the job involves supervision and your past experience has NOT, some general reading in supervisory methods and practices, particularly in the field of human relations, might be useful. Do NOT study agency procedures or detailed manuals. The oral board will be testing your understanding and capacity, not your memory.

5) Get a good night's sleep and watch your general health and mental attitude

You will want a clear head at the interview. Take care of a cold or any other minor ailment, and of course, no hangovers.

What should be done on the day of the interview?

Now comes the day of the interview itself. Give yourself plenty of time to get there. Plan to arrive somewhat ahead of the scheduled time, particularly if your appointment is in the fore part of the day. If a previous candidate fails to appear, the board might be ready for you a bit early. By early afternoon an oral board is almost invariably behind schedule if there are many candidates, and you may have to wait. Take along a book or magazine to read, or your application to review, but leave any extraneous material in the waiting room when you go in for your interview. In any event, relax and compose yourself.

The matter of dress is important. The board is forming impressions about you – from your experience, your manners, your attitude, and your appearance. Give your personal appearance careful attention. Dress your best, but not your flashiest. Choose conservative, appropriate clothing, and be sure it is immaculate. This is a business interview, and your appearance should indicate that you regard it as such. Besides, being well groomed and properly dressed will help boost your confidence.

Sooner or later, someone will call your name and escort you into the interview room. *This is it.* From here on you are on your own. It is too late for any more preparation. But remember, you asked for this opportunity to prove your fitness, and you are here because your request was granted.

What happens when you go in?

The usual sequence of events will be as follows: The clerk (who is often the board stenographer) will introduce you to the chairman of the oral board, who will introduce you to the other members of the board. Acknowledge the introductions before you sit down. Do not be surprised if you find a microphone facing you or a stenotypist sitting by. Oral interviews are usually recorded in the event of an appeal or other review.

Usually the chairman of the board will open the interview by reviewing the highlights of your education and work experience from your application – primarily for the benefit of the other members of the board, as well as to get the material into the record. Do not interrupt or comment unless there is an error or significant misinterpretation; if that is the case, do not hesitate. But do not quibble about insignificant matters. Also, he will usually ask you some question about your education, experience or your present job – partly to get you to start talking and to establish the interviewing "rapport." He may start the actual questioning, or turn it over to one of the other members. Frequently, each member undertakes the questioning on a particular area, one in which he is perhaps most competent, so you can expect each member to participate in the examination. Because time is limited, you may also expect some rather abrupt switches in the direction the questioning takes, so do not be upset by it. Normally, a board member will not pursue a single line of questioning unless he discovers a particular strength or weakness.

After each member has participated, the chairman will usually ask whether any member has any further questions, then will ask you if you have anything you wish to add. Unless you are expecting this question, it may floor you. Worse, it may start you off on an extended, extemporaneous speech. The board is not usually seeking more information. The question is principally to offer you a last opportunity to present further qualifications or to indicate that you have nothing to add. So, if you feel that a significant qualification or characteristic has been overlooked, it is proper to point it out in a sentence or so. Do not compliment the board on the thoroughness of their examination – they have been sketchy, and you know it. If you wish, merely say, "No thank you, I have nothing further to add." This is a point where you can "talk yourself out" of a good impression or fail to present an important bit of information. Remember, *you close the interview yourself*.

The chairman will then say, "That is all, Mr. _____, thank you." Do not be startled; the interview is over, and quicker than you think. Thank him, gather your belongings and take your leave. Save your sigh of relief for the other side of the door.

How to put your best foot forward

Throughout this entire process, you may feel that the board individually and collectively is trying to pierce your defenses, seek out your hidden weaknesses and embarrass and confuse you. Actually, this is not true. They are obliged to make an appraisal of your qualifications for the job you are seeking, and they want to see you in your best light. Remember, they must interview all candidates and a non-cooperative candidate may become a failure in spite of their best efforts to bring out his qualifications. Here are 15 suggestions that will help you:

1) Be natural – Keep your attitude confident, not cocky

If you are not confident that you can do the job, do not expect the board to be. Do not apologize for your weaknesses, try to bring out your strong points. The board is interested in a positive, not negative, presentation. Cockiness will antagonize any board member and make him wonder if you are covering up a weakness by a false show of strength.

2) Get comfortable, but don't lounge or sprawl

Sit erectly but not stiffly. A careless posture may lead the board to conclude that you are careless in other things, or at least that you are not impressed by the importance of the occasion. Either conclusion is natural, even if incorrect. Do not fuss with your clothing, a pencil or an ashtray. Your hands may occasionally be useful to emphasize a point; do not let them become a point of distraction.

3) Do not wisecrack or make small talk

This is a serious situation, and your attitude should show that you consider it as such. Further, the time of the board is limited – they do not want to waste it, and neither should you.

4) Do not exaggerate your experience or abilities

In the first place, from information in the application or other interviews and sources, the board may know more about you than you think. Secondly, you probably will not get away with it. An experienced board is rather adept at spotting such a situation, so do not take the chance.

5) If you know a board member, do not make a point of it, yet do not hide it

Certainly you are not fooling him, and probably not the other members of the board. Do not try to take advantage of your acquaintanceship – it will probably do you little good.

6) Do not dominate the interview

Let the board do that. They will give you the clues – do not assume that you have to do all the talking. Realize that the board has a number of questions to ask you, and do not try to take up all the interview time by showing off your extensive knowledge of the answer to the first one.

7) Be attentive

You only have 20 minutes or so, and you should keep your attention at its sharpest throughout. When a member is addressing a problem or question to you, give him your undivided attention. Address your reply principally to him, but do not exclude the other board members.

8) Do not interrupt

A board member may be stating a problem for you to analyze. He will ask you a question when the time comes. Let him state the problem, and wait for the question.

9) Make sure you understand the question

Do not try to answer until you are sure what the question is. If it is not clear, restate it in your own words or ask the board member to clarify it for you. However, do not haggle about minor elements.

10) Reply promptly but not hastily

A common entry on oral board rating sheets is "candidate responded readily," or "candidate hesitated in replies." Respond as promptly and quickly as you can, but do not jump to a hasty, ill-considered answer.

11) Do not be peremptory in your answers

A brief answer is proper – but do not fire your answer back. That is a losing game from your point of view. The board member can probably ask questions much faster than you can answer them.

12) Do not try to create the answer you think the board member wants

He is interested in what kind of mind you have and how it works – not in playing games. Furthermore, he can usually spot this practice and will actually grade you down on it.

13) Do not switch sides in your reply merely to agree with a board member

Frequently, a member will take a contrary position merely to draw you out and to see if you are willing and able to defend your point of view. Do not start a debate, yet do not surrender a good position. If a position is worth taking, it is worth defending.

14) Do not be afraid to admit an error in judgment if you are shown to be wrong

The board knows that you are forced to reply without any opportunity for careful consideration. Your answer may be demonstrably wrong. If so, admit it and get on with the interview.

15) Do not dwell at length on your present job

The opening question may relate to your present assignment. Answer the question but do not go into an extended discussion. You are being examined for a *new* job, not your present one. As a matter of fact, try to phrase ALL your answers in terms of the job for which you are being examined.

Basis of Rating

Probably you will forget most of these "do's" and "don'ts" when you walk into the oral interview room. Even remembering them all will not ensure you a passing grade. Perhaps you did not have the qualifications in the first place. But remembering them will help you to put your best foot forward, without treading on the toes of the board members.

Rumor and popular opinion to the contrary notwithstanding, an oral board wants you to make the best appearance possible. They know you are under pressure – but they also want to see how you respond to it as a guide to what your reaction would be under the pressures of the job you seek. They will be influenced by the degree of poise you display, the personal traits you show and the manner in which you respond.

ABOUT THIS BOOK

This book contains tests divided into Examination Sections. Go through each test, answering every question in the margin. We have also attached a sample answer sheet at the back of the book that can be removed and used. At the end of each test look at the answer key and check your answers. On the ones you got wrong, look at the right answer choice and learn. Do not fill in the answers first. Do not memorize the questions and answers, but understand the answer and principles involved. On your test, the questions will likely be different from the samples. Questions are changed and new ones added. If you understand these past questions you should have success with any changes that arise. Tests may consist of several types of questions. We have additional books on each subject should more study be advisable or necessary for you. Finally, the more you study, the better prepared you will be. This book is intended to be the last thing you study before you walk into the examination room. Prior study of relevant texts is also recommended. NLC publishes some of these in our Fundamental Series. Knowledge and good sense are important factors in passing your exam. Good luck also helps. So now study this Passbook, absorb the material contained within and take that knowledge into the examination. Then do your best to pass that exam.

EXAMINATION SECTION

EFFECTIVELY INTERACTING WITH AGENCY STAFF AND MEMBERS OF THE PUBLIC

Test material will be presented in a multiple-choice question format.

Test Task: You will be presented with a variety of situations in which you must apply knowledge of how best to interact with other people.

SAMPLE QUESTION:

A person approaches you expressing anger about a recent action by your department.
Which one of the following should be your first response to this person?
- A. Interrupt to say you cannot discuss the situation until he calms down.
- B. Say you are sorry that he has been negatively affected by your department's action.
- C. Listen and express understanding that he has been upset by your department's action.
- D. Give him an explanation of the reasons for your department's action.

The CORRECT answer to this sample question is Choice C.
Solution:

Choice A is not correct. It would be inappropriate to interrupt. In addition, saying that you cannot discuss the situation until the person calms down will likely aggravate the person further.

Choice B is not correct. Apologizing for your department's action implies that the action was improper.

Choice C is the correct answer to this question. By listening and expressing understanding that your department's action has upset the person, you demonstrate that you have heard and understand the person's feelings and point of view.

Choice D is not correct. While an explanation of the reasons for the action may be appropriate at a later time, at this moment the person is angry and would not be receptive to such an explanation.

EXAMINATION SECTION
TEST 1

DIRECTIONS: Each question or incomplete statement is followed by several suggested answers or completions. Select the one that BEST answers the question or completes the statement. *PRINT THE LETTER OF THE CORRECT ANSWER IN THE SPACE AT THE RIGHT.*

1. A group member who starts out at the same level as other group members and is able to move into a leadership position within that group would be described as what kind of a leader?
   A. Autocratic   B. Democratic   C. Emergent   D. Informal

   1.____

2. Your boss is only effective as the leader of your department when you and your coworkers are motivated experts on the topic at hand. If any of you do not really have expertise in a given field, his leadership falters somewhat. What type of leader is your boss?
   A. Laissez-faire   B. Technical   C. Democratic   D. Autocratic

   2.____

3. If a leader is in charge of an inexperienced group that does not have the appropriate information and proficiency to successfully complete a task, which of the following approaches should the leader use in order for success to follow within the group?
   A. Yelling   B. Delegating   C. Participating   D. Selling

   3.____

4. If you are a democratic leader, which of the following styles will be reflective of your leadership technique?
   A. Participating   B. Telling   C. Yelling   D. Delegating

   4.____

5. In producing equality in group member participation, which of the following should a leader NOT do?
   A. Make a statement or ask a question after each person in the group has said something
   B. Avoid taking a position during disagreements
   C. Limit comments to specific individuals within the group
   D. Control dominating speakers

   5.____

6. Social capital is BEST defined as
   A. social connections that help us make more money
   B. social connections that improve our lives
   C. a type of connection that experts believe is becoming more common in Europe than the United States.
   D. none of the above

   6.____

7. Communication is not simply sending a message. It is creating true
   A. connectivity   B. understanding
   C. empathy   D. power

   7.____

8. Of the following, which is NOT a part of the speech communication process?
   A. Feedback
   B. Central idea
   C. Interference
   D. Ethics

9. You are leading a meeting and afterwards your colleagues tell you they didn't quite understand what you were communicating verbally and nonverbally to them. Which part of the communication process do you need to work on?
   A. Channel
   B. Main idea
   C. Message
   D. Specific purpose

10. If nonverbal messages contradict verbal symbols, you are sending what kind of message to your public?
    A. Clear
    B. Mixed
    C. Controversial
    D. Negative

11. Which of the following would a public speaker use to deliver verbal symbols?
    A. Words
    B. Gestures
    C. Tone
    D. Facial expression

12. You are in the process of taking a course on interacting with the public. Your instructor starts talking about "the pathway" used to transmit a message. He explains that "the pathway" is better known as a
    A. link   B. loop   C. transmitter   D. channel

13. You finish an informational meeting with members of a community concerning a new park that will be built nearby. Afterwards, you are seeking feedback from them. Which of the following would NOT be a form of helpful feedback to you?
    A. Listeners raise their hands to point out a mistake
    B. Videotape the presentation
    C. Have colleagues and/or friends critique your presentation
    D. Hand out evaluation forms to listeners and have them fill it out after the presentation

14. Many public speaking experts have often repeated the famous quote, "A yawn is a silent _____," which references the quality of engagement within a presentation.
    A. rudeness   B. insult   C. shout   D. protest

15. If a child is running around during your speech and making a lot of noise, what type of interference would that be?
    A. Situational   B. External   C. Internal   D. Intentional

16. According to multiple recent surveys, of the five biggest mistakes that speakers make during a presentation, which one is the WORST?
    A. Being poorly prepared
    B. Trying to cover too much in one speech
    C. Failing to tailor a speech to the needs and interests of the audience
    D. Being boring

17. One of your colleagues has been asked to lead a meeting, and she confides in you that she suffers from excessive stage fright. Which of the following areas should you advise her to focus on to prevent her fear?
    A. Preparation
    B. Self-confidence
    C. Experience
    D. Sense of humor

18. When interacting with the public, which of the following elements should you NEVER imagine before engaging in public speaking?
    A. Effective delivery
    B. Nervousness
    C. Possibility of failure
    D. Success

19. A spokesperson is giving a speech to community members and you are evaluating him. You notice he tends to focus too much on himself and not enough on his audience. What is one piece of advice you can give him so he can shift his focus more to his audience?
    A. Change his amount of eye contact
    B. Work on facial expressions
    C. Alter his style of speaking
    D. All of the above

20. Most experts agree that the best way to eliminate excess energy would be to do all of the following EXCEPT
    A. using visual aids
    B. gripping the lectern
    C. walking to the right and left occasionally
    D. making gestures

21. A woman has lived in Newville her whole life. Recently, the Newville public works department made a policy change that angered her since it completely rearranged her schedule. She calls you on the phone and displays her displeasure with your department's recent policy change. What is the FIRST response you should have toward her?
    A. Interrupt her to say you cannot discuss the situation until she calms down
    B. Apologize to her that she has been negatively affected by the public works department
    C. Listen to her and demonstrate comprehension of her situation and why she was upset by your department's action
    D. Give her a detailed explanation of the reasons for the policy change

22. Which of the following is generally TRUE regarding public opinion?
    A. It is hard to move people toward a strong opinion on anything
    B. It is easy to move people toward a strong opinion on anything
    C. Most public relations are devoted to repairing negative public opinion about individuals
    D. It is easier than previously thought to move people away from an opinion they hold

23. Influencing a community member's attitude really comes down to which of the following?
    A. Journalism
    B. Public relations
    C. Social psychology
    D. Social action groups

24. If you attend a town hall meeting in which community members will bring up issues that require you to explain why your organization made the decisions it made, you will need to persuade them using evidence that is virtually indisputable. Which type of evidence should you stick to when explaining answers to the public?
    A. Facts
    B. Personal experience
    C. Emotions
    D. Using what appeals to the target public

25. In the last decade, especially after all the organizational and governmental scandals, public institutions must do which of the following in order to be successful?
    A. Work hard to earn and sustain favorable public opinion
    B. Trust the instincts expressed by the general public
    C. Be cognizant of the media's power
    D. Place the needs of the executives ahead of the needs of the public and other constituents

KEY (CORRECT ANSWERS)

1.	C		11.	A
2.	A		12.	D
3.	B		13.	A
4.	D		14.	C
5.	A		15.	B
6.	B		16.	C
7.	B		17.	A
8.	D		18.	B
9.	C		19.	D
10.	B		20.	B

21. C
22. D
23. B
24. A
25. A

TEST 2

DIRECTIONS: Each question or incomplete statement is followed by several suggested answers or completions. Select the one that BEST answers the question or completes the statement. *PRINT THE LETTER OF THE CORRECT ANSWER IN THE SPACE AT THE RIGHT.*

1. Unique attributes of the Internet that people can enjoy include all of the following EXCEPT 1.____
   A. immediacy
   B. low cost
   C. pervasiveness
   D. value for building one-to-one human relationships

2. Which of the following is a reason that social media can be more effective than traditional means of advertising and communication? 2.____
   A. When someone mentions your brand in social media, there is much more potential for other people to notice
   B. It is easier to decipher tone and purpose through Twitter or Facebook than through personal communication
   C. Most of the people who would be interested in your brand or service are comfortable and familiar with using social media
   D. Almost anyone can step into a media relations role if primarily using social media, because it is easy to communicate effectively through social media platforms

3. You are tasked with building publicity for the upcoming reveal of a new art installation in the town you work in. Your boss tells you to contact journalists, reporters and bloggers to help spread the word. Which of the following would be the MOST effective way of getting the media to help build coverage? 3.____
   A. Send out a mass e-mail to any media members in the area detailing the art installation and why you need coverage for it
   B. Call each media outlet and find out who would most likely cover and build publicity for your project. Then reach out to them either face-to-face or through a phone call
   C. Using Twitter, tweet at the media members and introduce yourself and your art installation and ask them to help spread the word
   D. None of the above

4. When using written communication, which of the following is a MAJOR challenge of writing to listeners? 4.____
   A. Providing lots of statistics
   B. Grabbing the attention of the listener quickly
   C. Providing information that is easily reviewed
   D. Presenting lots of incidentals

5. In order to communicate well in writing, which of the following pieces of advice sounds good but doesn't actually help you?
   A. Write material for all audiences rather than focusing on one
   B. Think before writing
   C. Write simply and with clarity
   D. Write and rewrite until you have a polished, finished product

5.____

6. You send out a public newsletter that details a project that your team is currently working on. One week later, an employee on your team tells you she has received multiple phone calls from confused constituents claiming that the newsletter's readability was low. When you send out a corrected newsletter, you need to make sure that your communication is easy to
   A. read   B. hear   C. edit   D. comprehend

6.____

7. You work for a biomedical company as a public outreach advocate. One day, an exciting e-mail circulates internally that states one of your scientists has discovered a cure for leukemia and your supervisor tasks you with writing the release. When writing the release, the newsworthy element inherent in the story is
   A. oddity   B. conflict   C. impact   D. proximity

7.____

8. When communicating with the public through the Internet, news releases
   A. should not be sent via e-mail   B. should be succinct
   C. should be sent via "snail mail"   D. none of the above

8.____

9. What is the MAJOR advantage of organizational publications? Their ability to
   A. give sponsoring organizations a means of uncontrolled communications
   B. deliver specific, detailed information to narrowly defined target publics
   C. avoid the problems typically associated with two-way media
   D. provide a revenue source for sponsoring organizations

9.____

10. You are confronted by a question from a reporter that you do not know the answer to. What should you do?
    A. Give them other information you are certain is right
    B. Tell them that information is "off the record" and will be distributed later
    C. Say "no comment" rather than look like you're uninformed
    D. Admit that you don't know but promise to provide the information later

10.____

11. Often times, an organization will run situation analysis before they share information with the public. Which one of these "internal factors" is usually associated with a situational analysis?
    A. A communication audit   B. Community focus groups
    C. A list of media contacts   D. Strategy suggestions

11.____

12. When you are hired, your first task is to start a process of identifying who are involved and affected by a situation central to your organization. This process is MOST commonly referred to as a(n)
    A. situation interview
    B. communication audit
    C. exploratory survey
    D. stakeholder analysis

13. Once a public outreach plan is in the summative evaluation phase, which of the following is generally associated with it?
    A. Impact
    B. Implementation
    C. Attitude change
    D. Preparation

14. Which of the following Internet-related challenges is MOST significant in the public relations field?
    A. Finding stable, cost-effective internet provides
    B. Representing clients using new social media environments
    C. Staying abreast of changing technology
    D. Training staff to use social media

15. Which of the following BEST defines a public issue? Any
    A. problem that brings a public lawsuit
    B. concern that is of mutual distress to competitors
    C. issue that is of mutual concern to an organization and its stakeholders
    D. problem that is not a concern to an organization and/or one of its stakeholders

16. A handful of people are posting misleading and/or negative information about your organization. What is the MOST proactive approach to handling this situation?
    A. Buy up enough shares in the site where the negative posts are, and prevent those users from posting again
    B. Post anonymous comments on the sites to help combat the negativity
    C. Prepare news releases that discredit the inaccuracies
    D. Make policy changes to address complaints highlighted on the sites

17. Your supervisor has recently asked you to review present and future realities for interacting with the public. Why is it important to continually review these?
    A. It helps develop your vision statement
    B. It helps interpret trends for management
    C. It helps construe the organization's business plan
    D. To know what path the company should pursue

18. You are the community relations director for the public water utility plant that has been the focus of a group of activists who are opposed to the addition of fluoride to drinking water. These objectors are not only at the plant each day, but they are also very active on social media inciting negativity towards the practice. As the director of the plant, you have overwhelming evidence that contradicts what the protestors are arguing. You want to combat their social media with your own internet plan. Which of the following is the MOST appropriate action for you to take?
    A. Use utility employees to write the blog, posing as healthcare professionals
    B. Reach out to medical professionals to volunteer to tweet and message community members under their own identities, but with no reference to the utility company
    C. Write a blog yourself, identifying yourself as an employee, and quote the scientific opinions of a variety of sources
    D. Pay for medical professionals to respond through the internet, identifying the utility as their sponsor, but without disclosing the compensation

19. You have recently completed an advertising campaign to help assuage the anger of the community at changes in the upcoming summer program for the city. Which of the following measurements would be MOST effective for evaluating the campaign's impact on audience attitude?
    A. A content analysis of media coverage
    B. Studying blog postings about the issue
    C. Analyzing pre- and post-numbers of people signed up for the summer programs
    D. Conducting a pre- and post-analysis of public opinions

20. In order to measure how policy changes will affect the public, you recommend that your supervisors first run a focus group for research. They like the idea, but want you to be in charge of running the group. Which of the following should you keep in mind as you form the focus group?
    A. Participants need to be randomly selected
    B. Make sure participants are radically different from one another so you get a range of opinions
    C. Include at least seven or more people in the group. Otherwise, the sample is too small to draw any conclusions.
    D. Formulate a research plan and use it as a script so you can make sure the results are ones that will work for you and your supervisors

21. The public university has recently come under fire for not offering enough tuition savings options for students. You have been hired to help promote the programs they offer including new savings programs. What is the MOST appropriate first step for you to take?
    A. Research pricing and development costs for the services
    B. Develop a survey to discover which factors impact families' savings
    C. Conduct a situation analysis to gain better understanding of the issues
    D. Hold a focus group to determine which messages would be most effective for your program

5 (#2)

22. After receiving feedback from the public on a new program, you are concerned 22.____
the results have been tainted by courtesy bias. You plan on sending out a new
questionnaire, but you need to make sure the bias is discouraged in it. Which
of the following techniques will be MOST effective at decreasing the partiality?
    A. Make questionnaire responses confidential
    B. Employ an outside firm to run the survey
    C. Offer a larger range of responses in the survey
    D. Both "A" and "C"

23. You have just relocated from Omaha, Nebraska to a branch in Chicago, Illinois. 23.____
In order to communicate well while in Chicago, you must remember that
    A. most publics have the same needs
    B. all publics are most interested only in technology you are using
    C. each audience has its own special needs and require different types of
       communication
    D. all audiences' needs overlap

24. Recently, the Parks and Recreation Department has come under fire 24.____
because it has been accused of too much marketing and not enough public
relations. Which of the following, if true, would lend credibility to these
accusations?
    A. Employees are focused on signing citizens up for as many different
       camps and activities available over the summer as possible
    B. Management consistently tries to send appreciation gifts to members of
       the community when they have volunteered or attending an activity
       sponsored by the Park district
    C. Weekly meetings are held to determine how to best improve the Park
       district's image as it relates to consumers
    D. Parks and Recreation is primarily focused on making sure the public
       enjoys their activities and trusts them to put on educational programs for
       the children

25. During your speech, a community member stands up and accuses you of 25.____
"spinning" a story. Which of the following BEST describes their accusation?
    A. You are relating a message through an agreed-upon ethical practice
       within the public relations community
    B. You are twisting a message to create performance where there is none
    C. You are trying to preserve hard-earned credibility
    D. You are providing the media with balanced and accurate information

KEY (CORRECT ANSWERS)

1. D
2. A
3. C
4. B
5. D

6. D
7. C
8. B
9. B
10. D

11. A
12. D
13. A
14. C
15. C

16. B
17. A
18. C
19. D
20. A

21. C
22. D
23. C
24. A
25. B

TEST 3

DIRECTIONS: Each question or incomplete statement is followed by several suggested answers or completions. Select the one that BEST answers the question or completes the statement. *PRINT THE LETTER OF THE CORRECT ANSWER IN THE SPACE AT THE RIGHT.*

1. In order to be successful in relating to the public, all of the following are vital EXCEPT
   A. performance
   B. relationship building
   C. formal education
   D. diversity of experience

   1.____

2. Which of the following is TRUE of communicating well regarding public relations experts?
   A. It will differentiate you and your role from others with special skills in the organization you work for
   B. It should be handled delicately in order to avoid upsetting stakeholders
   C. It is not as important as looking fashionable
   D. It is less important than understanding bureaucratic peculiarities

   2.____

3. You are critiquing a staffer who will lead an important meeting in two days and you note that she keeps using words that are steeped with connotation. You tell her to be careful of these words. Why?
   A. They transmit meaning too clearly, and you always want to leave wiggle room in your meaning
   B. They transmit the dictionary definition of a word that makes for a boring presentation
   C. They transmit meaning with an emotional overtone that could lead to misunderstanding in an overall message
   D. They lend themselves to stereotyping

   3.____

4. If you are trying to avoid biasing your intended audience, which of the following factors could help with that?
   A. Symbols
   B. Objective reporting by media
   C. Semantics
   D. Peers

   4.____

5. Of the following, which trait is MOST desirable when working with the public?
   A. Having the "gift for gab"
   B. Being an elite strategist
   C. Being able to leap organizational boundaries
   D. Performing well, especially in crises

   5.____

6. Which of the following areas is likely to see continual growth in the practice of public relations?
   A. Healthcare
   B. Social media
   C. Law enforcement
   D. None of the above

   6.____

7. What is the MOST commonly used public relations tactic?
   A. A news release
   B. A special event
   C. A PSA (public service announcement)
   D. A full feature news article

8. You have just been assigned to help with a new advertising campaign that will promote the new services offered by your organization. One major component of the new campaign will focus on publicity through photographs. Knowing you need to get this part of the project right, which of the following is the BEST tip to remember when taking PR photos?
   A. Don't use action shots because they usually wind up blurry
   B. Make sure there is good contrast and sharp detail
   C. Ensure that the product/services are the biggest thing(s) in the photo
   D. Photograph multiple people rather than only one

9. Which of the following situations would merit holding a press conference?
   A. When a corporation is restructured
   B. When a new public relations employee has been hired
   C. When information is of minor relevance to a specific audience
   D. When there is a new product to be released

10. On average, how long should an announcement to the public last on the radio?
    A. 2 minutes   B. 20 seconds   C. 1 minute   D. 10 seconds

11. In educating the public, you need to develop a PR plan and analyze each situation that could arise. Which of the following should NOT be a part of the analysis?
    A. Research
    B. Message crafting
    C. Creating a problem statement
    D. Asking the 5 W's and the H

12. You are in charge of promoting an event in the near future, but social media is unavailable to you at this time. Which of the following is the BEST way to get your message out to the media and, therefore, the public?
    A. An Op-Ed piece in the local newspaper
    B. A press conference
    C. A newsletter
    D. A news release

13. In the past few months, you and your colleagues have been accused of "doublespeak". Which of the following excerpts from presentations you have used could you defend and explain why it would NOT be an example of "doublespeak"?
    A. You called combat "fighting"
    B. Fred referred to genocide as "ethnic cleansing"
    C. Your boss referred to recent layoffs as "downsizing"
    D. Susie called the janitor a "custodial engineer"

14. In relating to the public, which of the following reflects key words in defining modern day PR?
    A. Deliberate, public interest, management function
    B. Persuasive, manipulative, improvisation
    C. Management, technical, flexible
    D. Influential, creative, evaluative

    14.____

15. How is educating and relating to the public different from being a journalist, marketing agent, or advertiser?
    A. It is more focused on advocacy
    B. It is about getting "free" press coverage
    C. It is about building relationships with various demographics
    D. All of the above

    15.____

16. Of the following, what is the BEST tactic for learning employee attitudes?
    A. Internal communications audit   B. Research
    C. Conference meeting   D. Both A and B

    16.____

17. When releasing news to the public, you should make sure it reads at a _____-grade reading level.
    A. 5th   B. 12th   C. 9th   D. 7th

    17.____

18. If you are using a euphemism that actually changes the meaning/impact of a concept you are trying to relay, what is that called?
    A. Insider language   B. Doublespeak
    C. Stylizing   D. Plagiarism

    18.____

19. Which of the following should be included in a public relations campaign if you want to ensure people will hear, understand, and believe your message?
    A. Repetition   B. Imagery
    C. Thoroughness   D. Acceptance

    19.____

20. In PR, what is it called when you track coverage and compare it over a period of time?
    A. Bookmarking   B. Benchmarking
    C. Comparison analysis   D. Correspondence

    20.____

21. What is a baseline study PRIMARILY used for?
    A. To determine changes in audience perception and attitude
    B. To figure out how well your company is doing in the marketplace compared to your competitors
    C. To find out the cost of buying space taken up by a particular article if that article is an advertisement
    D. None of the above

    21.____

22. Of the following people, who would BEST be considered a modern role model for successful public relations?
    A. Phineas T. Barnum (Barnum and Bailey)
    B. Ivy Lee
    C. Andrew Jackson
    D. Sir Walter Raleigh

23. If your organization has recently participated in a "publicity stunt," what type of PR strategy have you just used?
    A. Community
    B. Lobbying
    C. News management
    D. Crisis management

24. You tell your supervisor that you want to start using video press releases. When he presses you to explain why, you tell him that you want to take advantage of the fact that
    A. many news agencies don't review them ahead of broadcasting
    B. most reporters hired to create them have contacts within the industry
    C. they cover stories that some local news organizations cannot
    D. the production value may be better than those at local stations

25. A _____ is a type of news leak in which the source reveals large policy changes are on the table.
    A. disclosure   B. hook   C. exclusive   D. trial balloon

KEY (CORRECT ANSWERS)

1.	C		11.	B
2.	B		12.	D
3.	C		13.	A
4.	B		14.	A
5.	D		15.	D
6.	B		16.	D
7.	A		17.	C
8.	B		18.	B
9.	D		19.	A
10.	C		20.	B

21. A
22. B
23. C
24. C
25. D

TEST 4

DIRECTIONS: Each question or incomplete statement is followed by several suggested answers or completions. Select the one that BEST answers the question or completes the statement. *PRINT THE LETTER OF THE CORRECT ANSWER IN THE SPACE AT THE RIGHT.*

1. The Facial Feedback Hypothesis is a popular nonverbal theory that is BEST defined as
    A. people mirroring each other's facial expressions
    B. emotions leading to certain facial expressions
    C. facial expression can lead to the experience of certain emotions
    D. looking into a mirror while making a facial expression can cause one to change their facial expression

1._____

2. Of the following, which is NOT recognized as a function of smiling?
    A. It provides feedback.
    B. It signals disinterest.
    C. It helps establish rapport.
    D. It signals attentiveness.

2._____

3. When facial expressions are limited by cultural expectations, that is referred to as
    A. display rules
    B. syntactic displays
    C. adaptors
    D. interaction intensification

3._____

4. Of the following, which is recognized as part of the six basic emotions across cultures globally?
    A. Guilt
    B. Happiness
    C. Fear
    D. Both B and C

4._____

5. Which kinds of communication scenarios are more likely to see leadership roles develop from?
    A. Small group
    B. Intrapersonal communication
    C. Face-to-face public communication
    D. Text messaging

5._____

6. Which of the following highlights the key difference between small group communication and organizational communication?
    A. Feedback is easier and more immediate in organizational.
    B. Communication is more informal in small group communication.
    C. The message is easier to adapt to the specific needs of the receiver in organizational communication.
    D. People are more spread out in small group communication.

6._____

7. Which of the following would be an example of mediated communication?
    A. A principal addresses the student body in a speech.
    B. Two friends communicate while they work together in class.
    C. An employee texts his coworkers to see if they want to hang out after work.
    D. Three friends joke with one another while attending a concert.

7._____

8. Which of the following is FALSE concerning the way interpersonal relationships can affect us physically?
   A. Without interpersonal relationships, we can become sick
   B. These interpersonal relationships are necessary for humans; according to most research, humans raised in isolation are less healthy than those raised with others
   C. Humans are not the only mammals that need relationships in order to survive and thrive
   D. Interpersonal relationships are necessary until about age 12, but not later in adulthood

8.____

9. Which of the following is a characteristic of public relationships as they compare to private relationships?
   A. Intrinsic rewards
   B. Normative rules
   C. Use of particularistic knowledge
   D. Small number of intimates

9.____

10. When someone asks how you know they were angry, it is likely they fall into which style of facial expressions?
    A. Withholder
    B. Revealer
    C. Frozen-affect expressor
    D. Unwitting expressor

10.____

11. The theory of expectancy violations is BEST defined as
    A. nonverbal behavior reciprocated based primarily on positive or negative valence and the perceived reward value of the other person
    B. the process of intimacy exchange within a dyad relationship
    C. a social rule that says we should repay in kind what another has provided us
    D. none of the above

11.____

12. If an employee has a very good idea of what is and is not socially acceptable in any given situation, which kind of linguistic competence is she strong in?
    A. Phonemic   B. Syntactic   C. Pragmatic   D. Semantic

12.____

13. Which of the following would NOT be considered sexist language?
    A. Although a girl, Sonia is very brave.
    B. A gorgeous model, Johnny also likes to use his surfboard on the weekends.
    C. Jimmy's brother is a male nurse.
    D. None; all are considered to be sexist.

13.____

14. What is it called when individual experience, and NOT conventional agreement, creates meaning?
    A. Small talk communication
    B. Denotative meaning
    C. Connotative meaning
    D. Self-reflexive communication

14.____

15. Which of the following kinds of communication do students spend the MOST time engaged in?
    A. Listening   B. Writing   C. Reading   D. Speaking

15.____

16. Which of the following would be evidence of active listening?
    A. Maintain eye contact
    B. Nodding and making eye contact
    C. Asking for clarification
    D. All of the above

17. When listening in an evaluative context, which of the following must be done for it to be considered successful?
    A. Precisely disseminate stimuli in a message
    B. Comprehend the intended meaning of a message
    C. Make critical assessments of the accuracy of the facts in a message
    D. All of the above

18. A friend visits one day and tells you she thinks her husband is cheating on her with his ex-wife. She tells you she doesn't know what to do because she can't imagine living without him. If you wanted to paraphrase, which of the following BEST exemplifies that?
    A. "You are feeling insecure because you don't have a very good relationship with your husband."
    B. "You're afraid your husband is seeing his ex-wife behind your back; you don't know what to do; and you can't live without him."
    C. "You're afraid that your husband may still have feelings for his ex-wife and you're afraid you'll lose him."
    D. "Don't worry; his ex-wife is not back with him. You're just being paranoid."

19. When we form impressions of others, when might the recency effect impact our assessments? If we
    A. focus on our own feelings instead of the feelings of others
    B. are motivated to be more accurate or expect to be held accountable for our own perceptions
    C. engage in self-monitoring of our behaviors
    D. employ the discounting rule

20. Which of the following BEST defines a "modal self"?
    A. The ideal person for a social order
    B. A person who does not go to extremes
    C. The kind of self valued in the 20th century but not the 21st century
    D. The person who monitors his own behavior in social situations

21. Which of the following is TRUE of today's society?
    A. People are less selfish than they have ever been.
    B. People spend most of their time trying to be a single, unitary self.
    C. People have many short-lived relationships leading to their notions of themselves changing easily.
    D. People try to be frugal, honorable, and self-sacrificing.

22. A man's childhood consisted of a dismissing attachment style. Which of the following behaviors will he MOST likely exhibit as an adult?
    A. Anxiousness and ambivalence
    B. Obsessive friendliness and dependence
    C. Autonomy and distance from others
    D. Rhetorical sensitivity

23. When practicing self-disclosure, which of the following is a good rule of thumb?
    A. Be sure to disclose more than your partner
    B. Reserve your most important disclosures for people you know well
    C. Ignore the style of disclosure; the only thing that is important is content
    D. All of the above

24. During your first meeting as project leader, you approach your group and inform them that John will serve as your assistant project leader. He will be responsible for chairing team meetings and establishing the agenda. When John is given this formal leadership position, what type of power does he have over the other members of the project?
    A. Legitimate   B. Reward   C. Expert   D. Punishment

25. If you bring an employee to lead a project because she is knowledgeable and skilled in the area the project focuses on, what type of power does she possess?
    A. Legitimate   B. Reward   C. Referent   D. Expert

KEY (CORRECT ANSWERS)

1. C
2. B
3. A
4. D
5. A

6. B
7. C
8. D
9. B
10. D

11. A
12. C
13. D
14. C
15. A

16. D
17. C
18. B
19. D
20. A

21. C
22. C
23. B
24. A
25. D

EXAMINATION SECTION
TEST 1

DIRECTIONS: Each question or incomplete statement is followed by several suggested answers or completions. Select the one that BEST answers the question or completes the statement. *PRINT THE LETTER OF THE CORRECT ANSWER IN THE SPACE AT THE RIGHT.*

1. When conducting a needs assessment for the purpose of education planning, an agency's FIRST step is to identify or provide
   A. a profile of population characteristics
   B. barriers to participation
   C. existing resources
   D. profiles of competing resources

   1.____

2. Research has demonstrated that of the following, the MOST effective medium for communicating with external publics is(are)
   A. video news releases   B. television
   C. radio   D. newspapers

   2.____

3. Basic ideas behind the effort to influence the attitudes and behaviors of a constituency include each of the following EXCEPT the idea that
   A. words, rather than actions or events, are most likely to motivate
   B. demands for action are a usual response
   C. self-interest usually figures heavily into public involvement
   D. the reliability of change programs is difficult to assess

   3.____

4. An agency representative is trying to craft a pithy message to constituents in order to encourage the use of agency program resources.
   Choosing an audience for such messages is easiest when the message
   A. is project- or behavior-based   B. is combined with other messages
   C. is abstract   D. has a broad appeal

   4.____

5. Of the following factors, the MOST important to the success of an agency's external education or communication programs is the
   A. amount of resources used to implement them
   B. public's prior experiences with the agency
   C. real value of the program to the public
   D. commitment of the internal audience

   5.____

6. A representative for a state agency is being interviewed by a reporter from a local news network. The representative is being asked to defend a program that is extremely unpopular in certain parts of the municipality.
   When a constituency is known to be opposed to a position, the MOST useful communication strategy is to present

   6.____

23

A. only the arguments that are consistent with constituents' views
B. only the agency's side of the issue
C. both sides of the argument as clearly as possible
D. both sides of the argument, omitting key information about the opposing position

7. The MOST significant barriers to effective agency community relations include
   I. widespread distrust of communication strategies
   II. the media's "watchdog" stance
   III. public apathy
   IV. statutory opposition

   The CORRECT answer is:
   A. I only   B. I and II   C. II and III   D. III and IV

8. In conducting an education program, many agencies use workshops and seminars in a classroom setting.
   Advantages of classroom-style teaching over other means of educating the public include each of the following, EXCEPT
   A. enabling an instructor to verify learning through testing and interaction with the target audience
   B. enabling hands-on practice and other participatory learning techniques
   C. ability to reach an unlimited number of participants in a given length of time
   D. ability to convey the latest, most up-to-date information

9. The _____ model of community relations is characterized by an attempt to persuade the public to adopt the agency's point of view.
   A. two-way symmetric   B. two-way asymmetric
   C. public information   D. press agency/publicity

10. Important elements of an internal situation analysis include the
    I. list of agency opponents   II. communication audit
    III. updated organizational almanac IV. stakeholder analysis

    The CORRECT answer is:
    A. I and II   B. I, II, and III   C. II and III   D. I, II, III and IV

11. Government agency information efforts typically involve each of the following objectives, EXCEPT to
    A. implement changes in the policies of government agencies to align with public opinion
    B. communicate the work of agencies
    C. explain agency techniques in a way that invites input from citizens
    D. provide citizen feedback to government administrators

12. Factors that are likely to influence the effectiveness of an educational campaign include the
    I. level of homogeneity among intended participants
    II. number and types of media used
    III. receptivity of the intended participants
    IV. level of specificity in the message or behavior to be taught

    The CORRECT answer is:
    A. I and II   B. I, II, and III   C. II and III   D. I, II, III, and IV

13. An agency representative is writing instructional objectives that will later help to measure the effectiveness of an educational program.
    Which of the following verbs, included in an objective, would be MOST helpful for the purpose of measuring effectiveness?
    A. Know   B. Identify   C. Learn   D. Comprehend

14. A state education agency wants to encourage participation in a program that has just received a boost through new federal legislation. The program is intended to include participants from a wide variety of socioeconomic and other demographic characteristics. The agency wants to launch a broad-based program that will inform virtually every interested party in the state about the program's new circumstances.
    In attempting to deliver this message to such a wide-ranging constituency, the agency's BEST practice would be to
    A. broadcast the same message through as many different media channels as possible
    B. focus on one discrete segment of the public at a time
    C. craft a message whose appeal is as broad as the public itself
    D. let the program's achievements speak for themselves and rely on word-of-mouth

15. Advantages associated with using the World Wide Web as an educational tool include
    I. an appeal to younger generations of the public
    II. visually-oriented, interactive learning
    III. learning that is not confined by space, time, or institutional association
    IV. a variety of methods for verifying use and learning

    The CORRECT answer is:
    A. I only   B. I and II   C. I, II, and III   D. I, II, II, and IV

16. In agencies involved in health care, community relations is a critical function because it
    A. serves as an intermediary between the agency and consumers
    B. generates a clear mission statement for agency goals and priorities
    C. ensures patient privacy while satisfying the media's right to information
    D. helps marketing professionals determine the wants and needs of agency constituents

17. After an extensive campaign to promote its newest program to constituents, an agency learns that most of the audience did not understand the intended message.
MOST likely, the agency has
   A. chosen words that were intended to inform, rather than persuade
   B. not accurately interpreted what the audience really needed to know
   C. overestimated the ability of the audience to receive and process the message
   D. compensated for noise that may have interrupted the message

18. The necessary elements that lead to conviction and motivation in the minds of participants in an educational or information program include each of the following, EXCEPT the _____ of the message.
   A. acceptability   B. intensity
   C. single-channel appeal D. pervasiveness

19. Printed materials are often at the core of educational programs provided by public agencies.
The PRIMARY disadvantage associated with print is that it
   A. does not enable comprehensive treatment of a topic
   B. is generally unreliable in term of assessing results
   C. is often the most expensive medium available
   D. is constrained by time

20. Traditional thinking on public opinion holds that there is about _____ percent of the public who are pivotal to shifting the balance and momentum of opinion—they are concerned about an issue, but not fanatical, and interested enough to pay attention to a reasoned discussion.
   A. 2   B. 10   C. 33   D. 51

21. One of the most useful guidelines for influencing attitude change among people is to
   A. invite the target audience to come to you, rather than approaching them
   B. use moral appeals as the primary approach
   C. use concrete images to enable people to see the results of behaviors or indifference
   D. offer tangible rewards to people for changes in behavior

22. An agency is attempting to evaluate the effectiveness of its educational program. For this purpose, it wants to observe several focus groups discussing the same program.
Which of the following would NOT be a guideline for the use of focus groups?
   A. Focus groups should only include those who have participated in the program.
   B. Be sure to accurately record the discussion.
   C. The same questions should be asked at each focus group meeting.
   D. It is often helpful to have a neutral, non-agency employee facilitate discussions.

23. Research consistently shows that _____ is the determinant most likely to make a newspaper editor run a news release.
    A. novelty   B. prominence   C. proximity   D. conflict

24. Which of the following is NOT one of the major variables to take into account when considering a population-needs assessment?
    A. State of program development   B. Resources available
    C. Demographics   D. Community attitudes

25. The FIRST step in any communications audit is to
    A. develop a research instrument
    B. determine how the organization currently communicates
    C. hire a contractor
    D. determine which audience to assess

KEY (CORRECT ANSWERS)

1.	A	11.	A
2.	D	12.	D
3.	A	13.	B
4.	A	14.	B
5.	D	15.	C
6.	C	16.	A
7.	D	17.	B
8.	C	18.	C
9.	B	19.	B
10.	C	20.	B

21. C
22. A
23. C
24. C
25. D

TEST 2

DIRECTIONS: Each question or incomplete statement is followed by several suggested answers or completions. Select the one that BEST answers the question or completes the statement. *PRINT THE LETTER OF THE CORRECT ANSWER IN THE SPACE AT THE RIGHT.*

1. A public relations practitioner at an agency has just composed a press release highlighting a program's recent accomplishments and success stories.
   In pitching such releases to print outlets, the practitioner should
   I. e-mail, mail, or send them by messenger
   II. address them to "editor" or "news director"
   III. have an assistant call all media contacts by telephone
   IV. ask reporters or editors how they prefer to receive them

   The CORRECT answer is:
   A. I and II   B. I and IV   C. II, III, and IV   D. III only

   1._____

2. The "output goals" of an educational program are MOST likely to include
   A. specified ratings of services by participants on a standardized scale
   B. observable effects on a given community or clientele
   C. the number of instructional hours provided
   D. the number of participants served

   2._____

3. An agency wants to evaluate satisfaction levels among program participants, and mails out questionnaires to everyone who has been enrolled in the last year.
   The PRIMARY problem associated with this method of evaluative research is that it
   A. poses a significant inconvenience for respondents
   B. is inordinately expensive
   C. does not allow for follow-up or clarification questions
   D. usually involves a low response rate

   3._____

4. A communications audit is an important tool for measuring
   A. the depth of penetration of a particular message or program
   B. the cost of the organization's information campaigns
   C. how key audiences perceive an organization
   D. the commitment of internal stakeholders

   4._____

5. The "ABCs" of written learning objectives include each of the following, EXCEPT
   A. Audience   B. Behavior   C. Conditions   D. Delineation

   5._____

6. When attempting to change the behaviors of constituents, it is important to keep in mind that
   I. most people are skeptical of communications that try to get them to change their behaviors
   II. in most cases, a person selects the media to which he exposes himself
   III. people tend to react defensively to messages or programs that rely on fear as a motivating factor
   IV. programs should aim for the broadest appeal possible in order to include as many participants as possible

   The CORRECT answer is:
   A. I and II   B. I, II and III   C. II and III   D. I, II, III, and IV

7. The "laws" of public opinion include the idea that it is
   A. useful for anticipating emergencies
   B. not sensitive to important events
   C. basically determined by self-interest
   D. sustainable through persistent appeals

8. Which of the following types of evaluations is used to measure public attitudes before and after an information/educational program?
   A. Retrieval study   B. Copy test
   C. Quota sampling   D. Benchmark study

9. The PRIMARY source for internal communications is(are) usually
   A. flow charts   B. meetings
   C. voice mail   D. printed publications

10. An agency representative is putting together informational materials—brochures and a newsletter—outlining changes in one of the state's biggest benefits programs.
    In assembling print materials as a medium for delivering information to the public, the representative should keep in mind each of the following trends:
    I. For various reasons, the reading capabilities of the public are in general decline
    II. Without tables and graphs to help illustrate the changes, it is unlikely that the message will be delivered effectively
    III. Professionals and career-oriented people are highly receptive to information written in the form of a journal article or empirical study
    IV. People tend to be put off by print materials that use itemized and bulleted (●) lists

    The CORRECT answer is:
    A. I and II   B. I, II and III   C. II and III   D. I, II, III, and IV

11. Which of the following steps in a problem-oriented information campaign would typically be implemented FIRST?
    A. Deciding on tactics
    B. Determining a communications strategy
    C. Evaluating the problem's impact
    D. Developing an organizational strategy

12. A common pitfall in conducting an educational program is to
    A. aim it at the wrong target audience
    B. overfund it
    C. leave it in the hands of people who are in the business of education, rather than those with expertise in the business of the organization
    D. ignore the possibility that some other organization is meeting the same educational need for the target audience

13. The key factors that affect the credibility of an agency's educational program include
    A. organization   B. scope
    C. sophistication   D. penetration

14. Research on public opinion consistently demonstrates that it is
    A. easy to move people toward a strong opinion on anything, as long as they are approached directly through their emotions
    B. easier to move people away from an opinion they currently hold than to have them form an opinion about something they have not previously cared about
    C. easy to move people toward a strong opinion on anything, as long as the message appeals to their reason and intellect
    D. difficult to move people toward a strong opinion on anything, no matter what the approach

15. In conducting an education program, many agencies use meetings and conferences to educate an audience about the organization and its programs. Advantages associated with this approach include
    I. a captive audience that is known to be interested in the topic
    II. ample opportunities for verifying learning
    III. cost-efficient meeting space
    IV. the ability to provide information on a wider variety of subjects

    The CORRECT answer is:
    A. I and II   B. I, III and IV   C. II and III   D. I, II, III and IV

16. An agency is attempting to evaluate the effectiveness of its educational programs. For this purpose, it wants to observe several focus groups discussing particular programs.
    For this purpose, a focus group should never number more than _____ participants.
    A. 5   B. 10   C. 15   D. 20

17. A _____ speech is written so that several agency members can deliver it to different audiences with only minor variations.
    A. basic   B. printed   C. quota   D. pattern

18. Which of the following statements about public opinion is generally considered to be FALSE?
    A. Opinion is primarily reactive rather than proactive.
    B. People have more opinions about goals than about the means by which to achieve them.
    C. Facts tend to shift opinion in the accepted direction when opinion is not solidly structured.
    D. Public opinion is based more on information than desire.

19. An agency is trying to promote its educational program.
    As a general rule, the agency should NOT assume that
    A. people will only participate if they perceive an individual benefit
    B. promotions need to be aimed at small, discrete groups
    C. if the program is good, the audience will find out about it
    D. a variety of methods, including advertising, special events, and direct mail, should be considered

20. In planning a successful educational program, probably the first and most important question for an agency to ask is:
    A. What will be the content of the program?
    B. Who will be served by the program?
    C. When is the best time to schedule the program?
    D. Why is the program necessary?

21. Media kits are LEAST likely to contain
    A. fact sheets   B. memoranda
    C. photographs with captions   D. news releases

22. The use of pamphlets and booklets as media for communication with the public often involves the disadvantage that
    A. the messages contained within them are frequently nonspecific
    B. it is difficult to measure their effectiveness in delivering the message
    C. there are few opportunities for people to refer to them
    D. color reproduction is poor

23. The MOST important prerequisite of a good educational program is an
    A. abundance of resources to implement it
    B. individual staff unit formed for the purpose of program delivery
    C. accurate needs assessment
    D. uneducated constituency

24. After an education program has been delivered, an agency conducts a program evaluation to determine whether its objectives have been met.
General rules about how to conduct such an education program valuation include each of the following, EXCEPT that it
   A. must be done immediately after the program has been implemented
   B. should be simple and easy to use
   C. should be designed so that tabulation of responses can take place quickly and inexpensively
   D. should solicit mostly subjective, open-ended responses if the audience was large

25. Using electronic media such as television as means of educating the public is typically recommended ONLY for agencies that
   I. have a fairly simple message to begin with
   II. want to reach the masses, rather than a targeted audience
   III. have substantial financial resources
   IV. accept that they will not be able to measure the results of the campaign with much precision

   The CORRECT answer is:
   A. I and II   B. I, II and III   C. II and IV   D. I, II, III and IV

KEY (CORRECT ANSWERS)

1.	B		11.	C
2.	C		12.	D
3.	D		13.	A
4.	C		14.	D
5.	D		15.	B
6.	B		16.	B
7.	C		17.	D
8.	D		18.	D
9.	D		19.	C
10.	A		20.	D

21.	B
22.	B
23.	C
24.	D
25.	D

READING COMPREHENSION
UNDERSTANDING AND INTERPRETING WRITTEN MATERIAL

EXAMINATION SECTION
TEST 1

DIRECTIONS: Each question or incomplete statement is followed by several suggested answers or completions. Select the one that BEST answers the question or completes the statement. *PRINT THE LETTER OF THE CORRECT ANSWER IN THE SPACE AT THE RIGHT.*

1. Custody in prison work used to be considered of such supreme importance that everything else was secondary. This statement implies MOST directly that

    A. formerly nothing was as important as custody in prison work
    B. formerly only custody was considered important in prison work
    C. today all aspects of prison work are considered equally important
    D. today reform of the prisoner is considered more important than custody

    1.____

2. Since the total inmate treatment and training program is conditioned largely by custody requirements, its success is almost wholly dependent on flexibility of custody classification and handling of prisoners.
Of the following, the MOST accurate statement based on the above statement is that the

    A. conditions of custody are completely dependent on the handling of inmates in accordance with their classification
    B. daily schedule at the institution should be flexible in order for the treatment and training program to succeed
    C. main factor influencing the inmate treatment and training program is the requirement for the proper safekeeping of inmates
    D. most important factor in the success of the treatment and training program is the cooperation of the inmates

    2.____

3. An officer's revolver is a defensive and not offensive weapon.
On the basis of this statement only, an officer should BEST draw his revolver to

    A. fire at an unarmed burglar
    B. force a suspect to confess
    C. frighten a juvenile delinquent
    D. protect his own life

    3.____

4. Prevention of crime is of greater value to the community than the punishment of crime. If this statement is accepted as true, GREATEST emphasis should be placed on

    A. malingering   B. medication
    C. imprisonment   D. rehabilitation

    4.____

5. The criminal is rarely or never reformed. Acceptance of this statement as true would mean that GREATEST emphasis should be placed on

    A. imprisonment   B. parole
    C. probation   D. malingering

    5.____

6. Physical punishment of prison inmates has been shown by experience not only to be ineffective but to be dangerous and, in the long run, destructive of good discipline. According to the preceding statement, it is MOST reasonable to assume that, in the supervision of prison inmates,

   A. a good correction officer would not use physical punishment
   B. it is permissible for a good correction officer to use a limited amount of physical punishment to enforce discipline
   C. physical punishment improves discipline temporarily
   D. the danger of public scandal is basic in cases where physical punishment is used

7. There is no clear evidence that criminals, as a group, differ from non-criminals in their basic psychological needs.
   On the basis of this statement, it is MOST reasonable to assume that criminals and non-criminals

   A. are alike in some important respects
   B. are alike in their respective backgrounds
   C. differ but slightly in all respects
   D. differ in physical characteristics

8. Neither immediate protection for the community nor long-range reformation of the prisoner can be achieved by prison personnel who express toward the offender whatever feelings of frustration, fear, jealousy, or hunger for power they may have.
   Of the following, the CHIEF significance of this statement for correction officers is that, in their daily work, they should

   A. be on the constant lookout for opportunities to prove their courage to inmates
   B. not allow deeply personal problems to affect their relations with the inmates
   C. not try to advance themselves on the job because of personal motives
   D. spend a good part of their time examining their own feelings in order to understand better those of the inmates

9. Since ninety-five percent of prison inmates are released, and a great majority of these within two to three years, a prison which does nothing more than separate the criminal from society offers little promise of real protection to society.
   Of the following, the MOST valid reference which may be drawn from the preceding statement is that

   A. once it has been definitely established that a person has criminal tendencies, that person should be separated for the rest of his life from ordinary society
   B. prison sentences in general are much too short and should be lengthened to afford greater protection to society
   C. punishment, rather than separation of the criminal from society, should be the major objective of a correctional prison
   D. when a prison system produces no change in prisoners, and the period of imprisonment is short, the period during which society is protected is also short

10. A great handicap to successful correctional work lies in the negative response of the general community to the offender. Public attitudes of hostility toward, and rejection of, an ex-prisoner can undo the beneficial effects of even an ideal correctional system.
Of the following, the CHIEF implication of this statement is that

   A. a friendly community attitude will insure the successful reformation of the ex-prisoner
   B. correctional efforts with most prisoners would generally prove successful if it were not for public hostility toward the former inmate
   C. in the long run, even an ideal correctional system cannot successfully reform criminals
   D. the attitude of the community toward an ex-prisoner is an important factor in determining whether or not an ex-prisoner reforms

10.____

11. While retribution and deterrence as a general philosophy in correction are widely condemned, no one raises any doubt as to the necessity for secure custody of some criminals.
Of the following, the MOST valid conclusion based on the preceding statement is that the

   A. gradual change in the philosophy of correction has not affected custody practices
   B. need for safe custody of some criminals is not questioned by anyone
   C. philosophy of retribution, as shown in some correctional systems, has led to wide condemnation of custodial practices applied to all types of criminals

11.____

Questions 12-13.

DIRECTIONS: Questions 12 and 13 are to be answered SOLELY on the basis of the information contained in the following paragraph.

Those correction theorists who are in agreement with severe and rigid controls as a normal part of the correctional process are confronted with a contradiction; this is so because a responsibility which is consistent with freedom cannot be developed in a repressive atmosphere. They do not recognize this contradiction when they carry out their programs with dictatorial force and expect convicted criminals exposed to such programs to be reformed into free and responsible citizens.

12. According to the above paragraph, those correction theorists are faced with a contradiction who

   A. are in favor of the enforcement of strict controls in a prison
   B. believe that to develop a sense of responsibility, freedom must not be restricted
   C. take the position that the development of responsibility consistent with freedom is not possible in a repressive atmosphere
   D. think that freedom and responsibility can be developed only in a democratic atmosphere

12.____

13. According to the above paragraph, a repressive atmosphere in a prison

   A. does not conform to present day ideas of freedom of the individual
   B. is admitted by correction theorists to be in conflict with the basic principles of the normal correctional process

13.____

C. is advocated as the best method of maintaining discipline when rehabilitation is of secondary importance
D. is not suitable for the development of a sense of responsibility consistent with freedom

14. To state the matter in simplest terms, just as surely as some people are inclined to commit crimes, so some people are prevented from committing crimes by the fear of the consequences to themselves.
Of the following, the MOST logical conclusion based on this statement is that

A. as many people are prevented from committing criminal acts as actually commit criminal acts
B. most men are not inclined to commit crimes
C. people who are inclined to violate the law are usually deterred from their purpose
D. there are people who have a tendency to commit crimes and people who are deterred from crime

15. Probation is a judicial instrument whereby a judge may withhold execution of a sentence upon a convicted person in order to give opportunity for rehabilitation in the community under the guidance of an officer of the court. According to the preceding statement, it is MOST reasonable to assume that

A. a person on probation must report to the court at least once a month
B. a person who has been convicted of crime is sometimes placed on probation by the judge
C. criminals who have been rehabilitated in the community are placed on probation by the court after they are sentenced
D. the chief purpose of probation is to make the sentence easier to serve

Questions 16-19.

DIRECTIONS: Questions 16 through 19 are to be answered SOLELY on the basis of the following passage.

Traditional correctional institutions do not change or redirect the behavior of many of their inmates. Few of these establishments are equipped with adequate resources to treat the social and psychological handicaps of their wards. Too often, far removed ideologically from the world to which its charges must return, the institution often compounds the problems its corrective mechanisms are intended to cure. Training school academic programs, for example, range from poor to totally inadequate and usually reinforce negative feelings toward future learning experiences. Vocational programs are frequently designed to benefit the institution without regard to the inmate, and the usual low-key common denominator *treatment* program scarcely begins to meet the needs of many offenders.

Most correctional institutions must mobilize their limited resources in time and talent for purposes other than the ever-present concern about runaways or escapes. No one could quarrel rationally with the need to safeguard the community and control the behavior of people who may be of danger to themselves or others. It is ridiculous and tragic, however, that an overstated security approach is still the rule for the bulk of our correctional population.

16. The passage states that inmates of traditional correctional institutions are LIKELY to   16.____
    A. develop belief in radical political ideologies
    B. experience conditions that produce no betterment
    C. give major attention to devising plans of escape
    D. desire vocational training unrelated to their individual potential

17. The passage indicates that traditional training school academic programs lead inmates to   17.____
    A. adjust to the institutional setting
    B. avoid later formal learning
    C. develop respect for the values of education
    D. request more practical, vocational training

18. The passage indicates that most traditional correctional institutions, because of their ideological distance from the realities of the outside world, are MOST likely to   18.____
    A. ignore the safety of the outside community
    B. favor a minority of the inmate population
    C. lack properly motivated staff
    D. increase the problems of inmates

19. The passage states that the strong custodial function in most correctional institutions is MOST likely to be   19.____
    A. accorded excessive emphasis
    B. aimed at incorrigible inmates only
    C. necessary to redirect inmate behavior
    D. resented by the outside community

Questions 20-22.

DIRECTIONS: Questions 20 through 22 are to be answered SOLELY on the basis of the following passage.

The most widely accepted argument in favor of the death penalty is that the threat of its infliction deters people from committing capital offenses. Of course, since human behavior can be influenced through fear, and since man tends to fear death, it is possible to use capital punishment as a deterrent. But the real question is whether individuals think of the death penalty BEFORE they act, and whether they are thereby deterred from committing crimes. If for the moment we assume that the death penalty does this to some extent, we must also grant that certain human traits limit its effectiveness as a deterrent. Man tends to be a creature of habit and emotion, and when he is handicapped by poverty, ignorance, and malnutrition, as criminals often are, he becomes notoriously shortsighted. Many violators of the law give little thought to the possibility of detection and apprehension, and often they do not even consider the penalty. Moreover, it appears that most people do not regulate their lives in terms of the pleasure and pain that may result from their acts.

Human nature is very complex. A criminal may fear punishment, but he may fear the anger and contempt of his companions or his family even more, and the fear of economic insecurity or exclusion from the group whose respect he cherishes may drive him to commit the most daring crimes. Besides, fear is not the only emotion that motivates man. Love, loyalty, ambition, greed, lust, anger, and resentment may steel him to face even death in the perpetration of crime, and impel him to devise the most ingenious methods to get what he wants and to avoid detection.

If the death penalty were surely, quickly, uniformly, publicly, and painfully inflicted, it undoubtedly would prevent many capital offenses that are being committed by those who do consider the punishment that they may receive for their crimes. But this is precisely the point. Certainly, the way in which the death penalty has been administered in the United States is not fitted to produce this result.

20. Of the following, the MOST appropriate title for the above passage is

    A. CAPITAL OFFENSES IN THE UNITED STATES
    B. THE DEATH PENALTY AS A DETERRENT
    C. HUMAN NATURE AND FEAR
    D. EMOTION AS A CAUSE OF CRIME

21. The above passage implies that the death penalty, as it has been administered in the United States,

    A. was too prompt and uniform to be effective
    B. deterred many criminals who considered the possible consequences of their actions
    C. prevented crimes primarily among habitual criminals
    D. failed to prevent the commission of many capital offenses

22. According to the above passage, many violators of the law are

    A. intensely concerned with the pleasure or pain that may result from their acts
    B. influenced primarily by economic factors
    C. not influenced by the opinions of their family or friends
    D. not seriously concerned with the possibility of apprehension

Questions 23-25.

DIRECTIONS: Questions 23 through 25 are to be answered SOLELY on the basis of the information contained in the following paragraph.

As a secondary aspect of this revolutionary change in outlook resulting from the introduction of group counseling into the adult correctional institution, there must evolve a new type of prison employee, the true correctional or treatment worker. The top management will have to reorient their attitudes toward subordinate employees, respecting and accepting them as equal participants in the work of the institution. Rank may no longer be the measure of value in the inmate treatment program. Instead, the employee will be valuable whatever his location in the prison hierarchy or administrative plan in terms of his capacity constructively to relate himself to inmates as one human being to another. In group counseling, all employees must consider it their primary task to provide a wholesome environment for personality growth for the inmates in work crews, cell blocks, clerical pools, or classrooms. The above does not mean that custodial care and precautions regarding the prevention of disorders or escapes are cast aside or discarded by prison workers. On the contrary, the staff will be more acutely aware of the costs to the inmates of such infractions of institutional rules. Gradually, it is hoped, these instances of uncontrolled responses to over-powering feelings by inmates will become much less frequent in the treatment institution, In general, men in group counseling provide considerably fewer disciplinary infractions when compared with a control group of those still on a waiting list to enter group counseling, and especially fewer than those who do not choose to participate. It is optimistically anticipated that some day men in prison may have the same attitudes toward the staff, the same security in expecting treatment as do patients in a good general hospital.

23. According to the above paragraph, under a program of group counseling in an adult correctional institution, that employee will be MOST valuable in the inmate treatment program who

    A. can establish a constructive relationship of one human being to another between himself and the inmate
    B. gets top management to accept him as an equal participant in the work of the institution
    C. is in contact with the inmate in work crews, cell blocks, clerical pools or classrooms
    D. provides the inmate with a proper home environment for wholesome personality growth

24. According to the above paragraph, an effect that the group counseling program is expected to have on the problem of custody and discipline in a prison is that the staff will

    A. be more acutely aware of the cost of maintaining strict prison discipline
    B. discard old and outmoded notions of custodial care and the prevention of disorders and escapes
    C. neglect this aspect of prison work unless proper safeguards are established
    D. realize more deeply the harmful effect on the inmate of breaches of discipline

25. According to the above paragraph, a result that is expected from the group counseling method of inmate treatment in an adult correctional institution is

    A. a greater desire on the part of potential delinquents to enter the correctional institution for the purpose of securing treatment
    B. a large reduction in the number of infractions of institutional rules by inmates
    C. a steady decrease in the crime rate
    D. the introduction of hospital methods of organization and operation into the correctional institution

KEY (CORRECT ANSWERS)

1. A
2. C
3. D
4. D
5. A

6. A
7. A
8. B
9. D
10. D

11. B
12. A
13. D
14. D
15. B

16. B
17. B
18. D
19. A
20. B

21. D
22. D
23. A
24. D
25. B

TEST 2

DIRECTIONS: Each question or incomplete statement is followed by several suggested answers or completions. Select the one that BEST answers the question or completes the statement. *PRINT THE LETTER OF THE CORRECT ANSWER IN THE SPACE AT THE RIGHT.*

Questions 1-7.

DIRECTIONS: Questions 1 through 7 are to be answered on the basis of the following paragraph.

FLAGGING RULES

When a track gang is going to work under flagging protection at a given location, the Desk Trainmaster of the division must be notified. Work on trainways must not be performed on operating tracks between 6:00 A.M. and 9:00 A.M., or between 4:00 P.M. and 7:00 P.M. A flagman must be selected from the list of flagmen qualified as such by the Assistant General Superintendent. No person acting as a flagman may be assigned any duties other than those of a flagman. For underground flagging signals, lighted lanterns must be used. Out of doors, flags at least 23" x 29" in dimensions must be used between sunrise and sunset. Moving a red light across the track is the prescribed stop signal under normal flagging conditions. Moving a white light up and down means proceed slowly. A red light must never be used to give a proceed signal. Moving a yellow light up and down is a signal to a motorman to proceed very slowly. On the track to be worked on, two yellow lights must be displayed at a point not less than 500 feet, nor more than 700 feet, in approach to the flagman's station. On any track where caution lights are displayed, one green light must be displayed a safe distance beyond the farthest point of work. Caution lights must be displayed on the right hand side of the track.

1. Before starting work on a track, the transit official who should be notified is the

    A. General Superintendent
    B. Assistant General Superintendent
    C. Desk Trainmaster
    D. Yardmaster

2. It is permissible to start work on an operating track at

    A. 8 A.M.   B. 11 A.M.   C. 8 P.M.   D. 6 P.M.

3. A flagman for a track gang MUST be selected from

    A. men on light duty   B. disabled men
    C. a list of qualified men   D. senior trackmen

4. The flagman who is protecting a working gang of trackmen

    A. should lend a hand when needed in heavy lifting
    B. should clean up the track area while awaiting trains
    C. must not be assigned to other duties
    D. can collect scrap iron while awaiting trains

5. The prescribed *stop* signal is given by moving a

    A. red light up and down   B. green light up and down
    C. red light across the tracks   D. green light across the tracks

6. The normal *proceed slowly* signal is given by moving a

   A. red light up and down
   B. white light up and down
   C. yellow light across the tracks
   D. green light across the tracks

7. Of the following, an ACCEPTABLE distance between a work area and the yellow lights is _____ feet.

   A. 300 B. 600 C. 800 D. 1,000

Questions 8-12.

DIRECTIONS: Questions 8 through 12 are to be answered on the basis of the following passage.

    The handling of supplies is an important part of correctional administration. A good deal of planning and organization is involved in purchase, stock control, and issue of bulk supplies to the cell-block. This planning is meaningless, however, if the final link in the chain -- the cell-block officer who is in charge of distributing supplies to the inmates -- does not do his job in the proper way. First, when supplies are received, the officer himself should immediately check them or should personally supervise the checking, to make sure the count is correct. Nothing but trouble will result if an officer signs for 200 towels and discovers hours later that he is 20 towels short. Did the 20 towels *disappear,* or did they never arrive in the first place? Second, all supplies should be locked up until they are actually distributed. Third, the officer must keep accurate records when supplies are issued. Complaints will be kept to a minimum if the officer makes sure that each inmate has received the supplies to which he is entitled, and if the officer can tell from his records when it is time to reorder to prevent a shortage. Fourth, the officer should either issue the supplies himself or else personally supervise the issuing. It is unfair and unwise to put an inmate in charge of supplies without giving him adequate supervision. A small thing like a bar of soap does not mean much to most people, but it means a great deal to the inmate who cannot even shave or wash up unless he receives the soap that is supposed to be issued to him.

8. Which one of the following jobs is NOT mentioned by the above passage as the responsibility of a cellblock officer?

   A. Purchasing supplies
   B. Issuing supplies
   C. Counting supplies when they are delivered to the cell-block
   D. Keeping accurate records when supplies are issued

9. The above passage says that supplies should be counted when they are delivered. Of the following, which is the BEST way of handling this job?

   A. The cellblock officer can wait until he has some free time, and then count them himself.
   B. An inmate can start counting them right away, even if the cellblock officer cannot supervise his work.
   C. The cellblock officer can personally supervise an inmate who counts the supplies when they are delivered.
   D. Two inmates can count them when they are delivered, supervising each other's work.

10. The above passage gives an example concerning a delivery of 200 towels that turned out to be 20 towels short. The example is used to show that

    A. the missing towels were stolen
    B. the missing towels never arrived in the first place
    C. it is impossible to tell what happened to the missing towels because no count was made when they were delivered
    D. it does not matter that the missing towels were not accounted for because it is never possible to keep track of supplies accurately

11. The MAIN reason given by the above passage for making a record when supplies are issued is that keeping records

    A. will discourage inmates from stealing supplies
    B. is a way of making sure that each inmate receives the supplies to which he is entitled
    C. will show the officer's superiors that he is doing his job in the proper way
    D. will enable the inmates to help themselves to any supplies they need

12. The above passage says that it is unfair to put an inmate in charge of supplies without giving him adequate supervision.
    Which of the following is the MOST likely explanation of why it would be *unfair* to do this?

    A. A privilege should not be given to one inmate unless it is given to all the other inmates too.
    B. It is wrong to make one inmate work when all the others can sit in their cells and do nothing.
    C. The cellblock officer should not be able to get out of doing a job by making an inmate do it for him.
    D. The inmate in charge of supplies could be put under pressure by other inmates to do them *special favors.*

Questions 13-17.

DIRECTIONS: Questions 13 through 17 are to be answered on the basis of the following passage.

The typical correction official must make predictions about the probable future behavior of his charges in order to make judgments affecting those individuals. In learning to predict behavior, the results of scientific studies of inmate behavior can be of some use. Most studies that have been made show that older men tend to obey rules and regulations better than younger men, and tend to be more reliable in carrying out assigned jobs. Men who had good employment records on the outside also tend to be more reliable than men whose records show haphazard employment or unemployment. Oddly enough, men convicted of crimes of violence are less likely to be troublemakers than men convicted of burglary or other crimes involving stealth. While it might be expected that first offenders would be much less likely to be troublemakers than men with previous convictions, the difference between the two groups is not very great. It must be emphasized, however, that predictions based on a man's background are only likelihoods -- they are never certainties. A successful correction officer learns to give some weight to a man's background, but he should rely even more heavily on his own personal judgment of the individual in question. A good officer will develop in time a kind of sixth sense about human beings that is more reliable than any statistical predictions.

13. The above passage suggests that knowledge of scientific studies of inmate behavior would PROBABLY help the correction officer to

    A. make judgments that affect the inmates in his charge
    B. write reports on all major infractions of the rules
    C. accurately analyze how an inmate's behavior is determined by his background
    D. change the personalities of the individuals in his charge

14. According to the information in the above passage, which one of the following groups of inmates would tend to be MOST reliable in carrying out assigned jobs?

    A. Older men with haphazard employment records
    B. Older men with regular employment records
    C. Younger men with haphazard employment records
    D. Younger men with regular employment records

15. According to the information in the above passage, which of the following are MOST likely to be troublemakers?

    A. Older men convicted of crimes of violence
    B. Younger men convicted of crimes of violence
    C. Younger men convicted of crimes involving stealth
    D. First offenders convicted of crimes of violence

16. The above passage indicates that information about a man's background is

    A. a sure way of predicting his future behavior
    B. of no use at all in predicting his future behavior
    C. more useful in predicting behavior than a correction officer's expert judgment
    D. less reliable in predicting behavior than a correction officer's expert judgment

17. The above passage names two groups of inmates whose behavior might be expected to be quite different, but who in fact behave only slightly differently.
    These two groups are

    A. older men and younger men
    B. first offenders and men with previous convictions
    C. men with good employment records and men with records of haphazard employment or unemployment
    D. men who obey the rules and men who do not

Questions 18-22.

DIRECTIONS: Questions 18 through 22 are to be answered on the basis of the following passage.

A large proportion of the people who are behind bars are not convicted criminals, but people who have been arrested and are being held until their trial in court. Experts have often pointed out that this detention system does not operate fairly. For instance, a person who can afford to pay bail usually will not get locked up. The theory of the bail system is that the person will make sure to show up in court when he is supposed to since he knows that otherwise he will forfeit his bail -- he will lose the money he put up. Sometimes a person who can show that he is a stable citizen with a job and a family will be released on *personal recognizance* (without bail). The result is that the well-to-do, the employed, and the family men can often avoid the detention system. The people who do wind up in detention tend to be the poor, the unemployed, the single, and the young.

18. According to the above passage, people who are put behind bars   18.____

    A. are almost always dangerous criminals
    B. include many innocent people who have been arrested by mistake
    C. are often people who have been arrested but have not yet come to trial
    D. are all poor people who tend to be young and single

19. The above passage says that the detention system works UNFAIRLY against people   19.____

    A. rich   B. married   C. old   D. unemployed

20. The above passage uses the expression *forfeit his bail*. Even if you have not seen the word *forfeit* before, you could figure out from the way it is used in the passage that *forfeiting* PROBABLY means _____ something.   20.____

    A. losing track of   B. giving up
    C. finding   D. avoiding

21. When someone is released on *personal recognizance,* this means that   21.____

    A. the judge knows that he is innocent
    B. he does not have to show up for a trial
    C. he has a record of previous convictions
    D. he does not have to pay bail

22. Suppose that two men were booked on the same charge at the same time, and that the same bail was set for both of them. One man was able to put up bail, and he was released. The second man was not able to put up bail, and he was held in detention. The reader of the above passage would MOST likely feel that this result is   22.____

    A. *unfair,* because it does not have any relation to guilt or innocence
    B. *unfair,* because the first man deserves severe punishment
    C. *fair,* because the first man is obviously innocent
    D. *fair,* because the law should be tougher on poor people than on rich people

Questions 23-25.

DIRECTIONS: Questions 23 through 25 are to be answered on the basis of the information contained in the following paragraph.

Group counseling may contain potentialities of an extraordinary character for the philosophy and especially the management and operation of the adult correctional institution. Primarily, the change may be based upon the valued and respected participation of the rank-and-file of employees in the treatment program. Group counseling provides new treatment functions for correctional workers. The older, more conventional duties and activities of correctional officers, teachers, maintenance foremen, and other employees, which they currently perform, may be fortified and improved by their participation in group counseling. Psychologists, psychiatrists, and classification officers may also need to revise their attitudes toward others on the staff and toward their own procedure in treating inmates to accord with the new type of treatment program which may evolve if group counseling were to become accepted practice in the prison. The primary locale of the psychological treatment program may move from the clinical center to all places in the institution where inmates are in contact with employees. The thoughtful guidance and steering of the program, figuratively its pilot-house, may still be the clinical center. The actual points of contact of the treatment program will, however, be wherever inmates are in personal relationship, no matter how superficial, with employees of the prison.

23. According to the above paragraph, a basic change that may be brought about by the introduction of a group counseling program into an adult correctional institution would be that the

    A. educational standards for correctional employees would be raised
    B. management of the institution would have to be selected primarily on the basis of ability to understand and apply the counseling program
    C. older and conventional duties of correctional employees would assume less importance
    D. rank-and-file employees would play an important part in the treatment program for inmates

24. According to the above paragraph, the one of the following that is NOT mentioned specifically as a change that may be required by or result from the introduction of group counseling in an adult correctional institution is a change in the

    A. attitude of the institution's classification officers toward their own procedures in treating inmates
    B. attitudes of the institution's psychologists toward correction officers
    C. place where the treatment program is planned and from which it is directed
    D. principal place where the psychological treatment program makes actual contact with the inmate

25. According to the above paragraph, under a program of group counseling in an adult correctional institution, treatment of inmates takes place

    A. as soon as they are admitted to the prison
    B. chiefly in the clinical center
    C. mainly where inmates are in continuing close and personal relationship with the technical staff
    D. wherever inmates come in contact with prison employees

KEY (CORRECT ANSWERS)

1. C
2. B
3. C
4. C
5. C

6. B
7. B
8. A
9. C
10. C

11. B
12. D
13. A
14. B
15. C

16. D
17. B
18. C
19. D
20. B

21. D
22. A
23. D
24. C
25. D

READING COMPREHENSION
UNDERSTANDING AND INTERPRETING WRITTEN MATERIAL
EXAMINATION SECTION
TEST 1

DIRECTIONS: Each question or incomplete statement is followed by several suggested answers or completions. Select the one that BEST answers the question or completes the statement. *PRINT THE LETTER OF THE CORRECT ANSWER IN THE SPACE AT THE RIGHT.*

Questions 1-3.

DIRECTIONS: Questions 1 through 3 are to be answered SOLELY on the basis of the following passage.

The basic disparity between punitive and correctional crime control should be noted. The first explicitly or implicitly assumes the availability of choice or freedom of the will and asserts the responsibility of the individual for what he does. Thus, the concept of punishment has both a moral and practical justification. However, correctional crime control, though also deterministic in outlook, either explicitly or implicitly considers criminal behavior as the result of conditions and factors present in the individual or his environment; it does not think in terms of free choices available to the individual and his resultant responsibility, but rather in terms of the removal of the criminogenic conditions for which the individual may not be responsible and over which he may not have any control. Some efforts have been made to achieve a theoretical reconciliation of these two rather diametrically opposed approaches but this has not been accomplished, and their coexistence in practice remains an unresolved contradiction.

1. According to the *correctional* view of crime control mentioned in the above passage, criminal behavior is the result of
   A. environmental factors for which individuals should be held responsible
   B. harmful environmental factors which should be eliminated
   C. an individual's choice for which he should be held responsible and punished
   D. an individual's choice and can be corrected in a therapeutic environment

1.____

2. According to the above passage, the one of the following which is a problem in correctional practice is
   A. identifying emotionally disturbed individuals
   B. determining effective punishment for criminal behavior
   C. reconciling the punitive and correctional views of crime control
   D. assuming that a criminal is the product of his environment and has no free will

2.____

3. According to the above passage, the one of the following which is an ASSUMPTION underlying the punitive crime control viewpoint rather than the correctional viewpoint is that crime is caused by

3.____

A. inherited personality traits
B. poor socio-economic background
C. lack of parental guidance
D. irresponsibility on the part of the individual

Questions 4-9.

DIRECTIONS: Questions 4 through 9 are to be answered SOLELY on the basis of the following passage.

Man's historical approach to criminals can be conveniently summarized as a succession of three R's: Revenge, Restraint, and Reformation. Revenge was the primary response prior to the first revolution in penology in the 18th and 19th centuries. It was replaced during that revolution by an emphasis upon restraint. When the second revolution occurred in the late 19th and 20th centuries, reformation became an important objective. Attention was focused upon the mental and emotional makeup of the offender and efforts were made to alter these as the primary sources of difficulty.
We have now entered yet another revolution in which a fourth concept has been added to the list of R's: Reintegration. This has come about because students of corrections feel that a singular focus upon reforming the offender is inadequate. Successful rehabilitation is a two-sided coin, including reformation on one side and reintegration on the other.
It can be argued that the third revolution is premature. Society itself is still very ambivalent about the offender. It has never really replaced all vestiges of revenge or restraint, simply supplemented them. Thus, while it is unwilling to kill or lock up all offenders permanently, it is also unwilling to give full support to the search for alternatives.

4. According to the above passage, revolutions against accepted treatment of criminals have resulted in all of the following approaches to handling criminals EXCEPT   4.____
   A. revenge   B. restraint   C. reformation   D. reintegration

5. According to the above passage, society NOW views the offender with   5.____
   A. uncertainty   B. hatred   C. sympathy   D. acceptance

6. According to the above passage, the second revolution directed PARTICULAR attention to   6.____
   A. preparing the offender for his return to society
   B. making the pain of punishment exceed the pleasure of crime
   C. exploring the inner feelings of the offender
   D. restraining the offender from continuing his life of crime

7. According to the above passage, students of corrections feel that the lack of success of rehabilitation programs is due to   7.____
   A. the mental and emotional makeup of the offender
   B. vestiges of revenge and restraint which linger in correction programs
   C. failure to achieve reintegration together with reformation
   D. premature planning of the third revolution

8. The above passage suggests that the latest revolution will
   A. fail and the cycle will begin again with revenge or restraint
   B. be the last revolution
   C. not work unless correctional goals can be defined
   D. succumb to political and economic pressures

9. The one of the following titles which BEST expresses the main idea of the above passage is
   A. IS CRIMINAL JUSTICE ENOUGH?
   B. APPROACHES IN THE TREATMENT OF THE CRIMINAL OFFENDER
   C. THE THREE R'S IN CRIMINAL REFORMATION
   D. MENTAL DISEASE FACTORS IN THE CRIMINAL CORRECTION SYSTEM

Questions 10-15.

DIRECTIONS: Questions 10 through 15 are to be answered SOLELY on the basis of the following passage.

In a study by J.E. Cowden, an attempt was made to determine which variables would best predict institutional adjustment and recidivism in recently committed delinquent boys. The results suggested in particular that older boys, when first institutionalized, who are initially rated as being more mature and more amenable to change, will most likely adjust better than the average boy adjusts to the institution. Prediction of institutional adjustment was rendered slightly more accurate by using the variables of age and personality prognosis in combined form.

With reference to the prediction of recidivism, boys who committed more serious offenses showed less recidivism than average. These boys were also older than average when first committed. The variable of age accounts in part for both their more serious offenses and for their lower subsequent rate of recidivism.

The results also showed some trends suggesting that boys from higher socio-economic b backgrounds tended to commit more serious offenses leading to their institutionalization as delinquents. However, neither the ratings of socio-economic status nor *home-environment* appeared to be significantly related to recidivism in this study.

Cowden also found an essentially linear relationship between personality prognosis and recidivism, and between institutional adjustment and recidivism. When these variables were used jointly to predict recidivism, accuracy of prediction was increased only slightly, but in general the ability to predict recidivism fell far below the ability to predict institutional adjustment.

10. According to the above passage, which one of the following was NOT found to be a significant factor in predicting recidivism?
    A. Age
    B. Personality
    C. Socio-economic background
    D. Institutional adjustment

11. According to the above passage, institutional adjustment was MORE accurately predicted when the variables used were
    A. socio-economic background and recidivism
    B. recidivism and personality
    C. personality and age
    D. age and socio-economic background

12. According to the above passage, which of the following were variables in predicting both recidivism and institutional adjustment? 12.____
    A. Age and personality
    B. Family background and age
    C. Nature of offense and age
    D. Personality

13. Which one of the following conclusions is MOST justified by the above passage? 13.____
    A. Institutional adjustment had a lower level of predictability and recidivism.
    B. Recidivism and seriousness of offense are negatively correlated to some degree.
    C. Institutional adjustment and personality prognosis, when considered together, are significantly better predictors of recidivism than either one alone.
    D. A delinquent boy from a lower class family background is more likely to have committed a serious first offense than a delinquent boy from a higher socio-economic background.

14. The study discussed in the above passage found that delinquent boys from a higher socio-economic background tended to 14.____
    A. commit more serious crimes
    B. commit less serious crimes
    C. show more recidivism than average
    D. show less recidivism than average

15. The MOST appropriate conclusion to be drawn from the study discussed above is that 15.____
    A. delinquent boys from higher socio-economic backgrounds show less institutional adjustment than average
    B. a high positive correlation was found between recidivism and institutional adjustment
    C. home environment, although not significantly related to recidivism, did influence institutional adjustment
    D. older boys are more likely to commit more serious first offenses and show less recidivism than younger boys

Questions 16-18.

DIRECTIONS: Questions 16 through 18 are to be answered SOLELY on the basis of the following passage.

Educational programming of the offender has become part of the dominant philosophy in the correctional community. Due to the recent increase in national funding for demonstration prison education projects, future research endeavors may well be facilitated so that we can better evaluate the effectiveness of specific educational approaches. Research on past programs has resulted in various conclusions as to their effectiveness in the reduction of recidivism. Even though some programs have seemed promising, when they are properly evaluated, the initial results have been found to be spurious. Invalidity stemmed, by and large, from the fact that inmates shown to be *successful* in such educational programs may have *had it made* anyway, particularly when those selected for the program were the best risks. Success of the program was judged on the basis of a study of recidivism which, due to lack of funds, was of insufficient duration.

Research is the bookkeeping of corrections. Unfortunately, many correctional enterprises operate without such bookkeeping. When this happens, like businesses without bookkeeping, they may soon be bankrupt. However, unlike business, corrections can provide a steady salary for its employees even when it is bankrupt.

Despite these sad conclusions, effective program implementation can become a reality through continued experimentation and evaluation, utilizing acceptable methodological procedures and specially trained personnel, as well as having the necessary total institutional support.

16. According to the above passage, the apparent success of past correctional educational programs was due in LARGE part to
    A. biased samples
    B. competent trainers
    C. societal acceptance
    D. inferior goals

16.____

17. The second paragraph in the above passage states that *Research is the bookkeeping of corrections.*
    Which of the following MOST accurately describes what is meant by this statement?
    A. Since correctional facilities are government institutions, only records of government research grants and the use of those grants can indicate when the institution is in financial difficulty.
    B. Research provides to correctional institutions information which is essential for their decision-making.
    C. Without grants for research, correctional institutions will become financially bankrupt even though they are still able to pay employee salaries.
    D. Correctional institutions must keep abreast of research or they will find themselves educationally bankrupt.

17.____

18. According to the above passage, the future of educational programming is brighter than its past because of
    A. social awareness
    B. longer programs
    C. increased national funding
    D. more highly qualified administrators

18.____

Questions 19-23.

DIRECTIONS: Questions 19 through 23 are to be answered SOLELY on the basis of the following passage.

The social problems created by the urban delinquent gang member require the attention and resources of the entire community. Recent studies have shown that we are dealing with a boy who early in life has his first official contact with the police and who, shortly afterwards, is bound for juvenile court. The gang member commits several delinquencies before reaching adult status and the earlier his onset of delinquency, the more serious become his violations of the law. There is also evidence of increasingly serious delinquency involvement of a substantial proportion of the gang members. Of major significance are the shorter periods of time between each succeeding offense and the delinquents; employment or threat to employ force and violence.

All of these findings testify to the urgent need for prevention and treatment to be directed at pre- and early adolescence and to be sensitive to the importance of the first signs of youthful disregard for society's legal norms. Follow-up studies on delinquent gang members revealed that forty percent of the gang members continued into adult crime. For several reasons, this is a minimal figure and should probably be twenty percent higher. It is reasonable to infer that, given more thorough follow-up techniques and a longer follow-up period, an appreciable number of those for whom no criminal records were located will acquire them. In any event, these studies have revealed a strong linkage between delinquency and crime. This linkage has been established by following up a group of gang members into adulthood rather than by tracing back a group of adult offenders into delinquency, and by utilizing a sample of juveniles dealt with by the police rather than those appearing before a juvenile court, or in a clinic.

19. According to the above passage, as delinquents get older, their crimes GENERALLY become _____ serious _____ frequent.
    A. more; and more
    B. more; but less
    C. less; but more
    D. less; and less

20. The above passage SUGGESTS that delinquents should receive
    A. severe punishment at the time of their first offense
    B. institutional care until such time that they may prove themselves capable of functioning in a free society
    C. treatment at pre- and early adolescence at the first signs of disregard for societal norms
    D. continuous psychological counseling from the time of their first offense until the delinquent reaches legal age

21. According to the above passage, delinquent gang members pose a problem which should be the responsibility of the
    A. community
    B. police
    C. courts
    D. social worker

22. According to the above passage, follow-up studies on delinquent gang members have underestimated the percent of gang members who continued to adult crime because
    A. their sample was biased as it only involved urban gang members
    B. the studies did not follow the *career* of the sample group for a long enough period of time
    C. the studies concerned only those juveniles who, as adults, were dealt with by the police and not those who appeared in court or were referred to a clinic
    D. the method used, that of following up a group of gang members rather than tracing back a group of adult offenders, was invalid

23. According to the above passage, the actual percent of delinquent gang members who continue into adult crime is MOST NEARLY
    A. 20%
    B. 40%
    C. 50%
    D. 60%

Questions 24-25.

DIRECTIONS: Questions 24 through 25 are to be answered SOLELY on the basis of the following passage.

The criminal justice system is generally regarded as having the basic objective of reducing crime. However, one must also consider its larger objective of minimizing the total social costs associated with crime and crime control. Both of these components are complex and difficult to measure completely. The social costs associated with crime come from the long- and short-term physical damage, psychological harm, and property losses to victims as a result of crimes committed. Crime also creates serious indirect effects. It can induce a feeling of insecurity that is only partially reflected in business losses and economic disruption due to anxiety about venturing into high crime rate areas.

Balanced against these costs associated with crime must be the consequences of actions taken to reduce them. Money spent on developing, maintaining, and operating criminal justice agencies is part of the cost of the crime control system. But there are also indirect costs, such as welfare payments to prisoners' families, income lost by offenders who are denied good jobs, legal fees, and wages lost by witnesses. In addition, there are penalties suffered by suspects erroneously arrested or sentenced, the limitation on personal liability resulting from police surveillance, and the invasion of privacy in maintaining criminal records.

24. According to the above passage, all of the following are indirect costs of the crime control system EXCEPT
    A. wages lost by witnesses
    B. money spent for legal services
    C. payments made to the families of prisoners
    D. money spent on operating criminal justice agencies

25. According to the above passage, actions taken to reduce crime
    A. will reduce the indirect costs of the crime control system
    B. may result in a decrease of personal liberty
    C. may cause psychological harm to victims of crime
    D. should immediately start improving the criminal justice system

KEY (CORRECT ANSWERS)

1.	B		11.	C
2.	C		12.	A
3.	D		13.	B
4.	A		14.	A
5.	A		15.	D
6.	C		16.	A
7.	C		17.	B
8.	C		18.	C
9.	B		19.	A
10.	C		20.	C

21. A
22. B
23. D
24. D
25. B

TEST 2

DIRECTIONS: Each question or incomplete statement is followed by several suggested answers or completions. Select the one that BEST answers the question or completes the statement. *PRINT THE LETTER OF THE CORRECT ANSWER IN THE SPACE AT THE RIGHT.*

Questions 1-4.

DIRECTIONS: Questions 1 through 4 are to be answered SOLELY on the basis of the following passage.

    The initial contact between the offender and the correctional social worker frequently occurs at the point of extreme crisis, when the usual adaptive mechanisms have been broken down. In many areas of correctional practice, such as probation and parole, this contact is often followed by long periods during which limited freedom is officially imposed. It is at such points that response to the offer of hope for restoring equilibrium may mean most, and that new coping capacities and new person-environment relationships develop. As a result, many correctional social workers have become skilled in strategies of crisis intervention. What they learn from such endeavors does not generally find its way into the professional literature; thus, the correctional social worker has contributed little to developing and testing practice theory. However, beginning efforts are being made to remedy this situation, and it is probable that corrections may provide an important laboratory from which tomorrow's understanding of the theory and strategies of crisis intervention will emerge.

1. Which of the following is the MOST appropriate title for the above passage?   1.____
    A. CORRECTIONAL SOCIAL WORK IN CRISIS
    B. CRISIS INTERVENTION AND CORRECTIONAL SOCIAL WORK
    C. COPING CAPACITIES OF PROBATIONERS AND PAROLEES
    D. THE THEORY AND PRACTICE OF CRISIS INTERVENTION

2. It can be concluded from the above passage that crisis intervention as a   2.____
   method of treatment and rehabilitation in correctional social work is based on the premise that a(n)
    A. offender may be more likely to respond to help and change his lifestyle a a time of crisis, such as being on probation or parole, when incarceration is the only other alternative
    B. person is not likely to respond to help and change his lifestyle unless he is in a crisis situation, such as being on probation or parole, when he is threatened by imprisonment
    C. offender sentenced to probation or parole is likely to respond to help and change his lifestyle, because his freedom is limited and supervision is imposed on him
    D. situation such as probation or parole, in which an offender is supervised and his freedom is limited, presents ideal conditions for constructive personality change

3. On the basis of the above passage, it would be VALID to assume that
   A. offenders sentenced to probation and parole usually develop coping capacities which would not emerge during imprisonment
   B. offenders who are rehabilitated as a result of probation and parole have greater coping capacities in crisis situations
   C. a life crisis situation such as being sentenced to probation or parole may become a positive force toward an offender's rehabilitation
   D. an offender's ability to develop new coping capacities in times of crisis should be a decisive factor in determining the recommended sentence

4. According to the above passage, correctional social workers' experiences in crisis intervention have
   A. encouraged use of crisis intervention strategy
   B. contributed to theory rather than practice
   C. not resulted in further learning
   D. not generally been reported in print

Questions 5-9.

DIRECTIONS: Questions 5 through 9 are to be answered SOLELY on the basis of the following passage.

The group worker must be concerned with two major goals in correctional treatment of juvenile offenders: (a) sustaining and reinforcing conventional value systems, and (b) enhancing the youth's positive self-image and general feeling of worthiness. The group processes involved in working toward these ends are so interrelated that treatment can meet both goals by improving interpersonal skills and experiences. As an initial concept, it is important to recognize that, in spite of delinquent behavior, adolescents usually do exhibit conscience formation, as may be seen in their support of conformity values, evidence of guilt and conventional behavior, and rationalization of delinquent behavior. It is this very ambivalence toward the conventional order that can be the basis for rehabilitation. On the basis of the distinction between real guilt and guilt reflecting emotional problems, an ideal therapeutic objective is to reach the point at which the internal and external controls are in general harmony and agency expectations are closely allied to and consistent with group and individual expectations.

5. Which of the following is the BEST title for the above passage?
   A. GROUP TREATMENT OF JUVENILE OFFENDERS
   B. THE GROUP WORKER AND CORRECTIONAL TREATMENT
   C. THE JUVENILE OFFENDER
   D. CONSCIENCE FORMATION IN JUVENILE OFFENDERS

6. On the basis of the above passage, it would be VALID to assume that group treatment of the juvenile offender can result in the development of
   A. greater self-confidence
   B. rationalization of delinquent behavior
   C. guilt and conscience formation
   D. increased conscientiousness

7. On the basis of the above statement, it would be VALID to conclude that juvenile offenders   7.____
   A. are anxious for rehabilitation
   B. have no internal or external controls
   C. are deficient in interpersonal skills and experiences
   D. feel more guilt because of emotional problems than because of offenses committed

8. According to the above passage, a characteristic of juvenile offenders which makes them amenable to correctional treatment is that they   8.____
   A. can be reached by group processes
   B. have a general feeling of worthiness
   C. show signs of conscience formation
   D. are ambivalent toward rehabilitation

9. According to the above passage, an IDEAL therapeutic objective in the group treatment of juvenile offenders would be based on   9.____
   A. agency expectations
   B. group expectations
   C. the distinction between real guilt and irrational guilt
   D. the harmony between external and internal controls

Questions 10-14.

DIRECTIONS: Questions 10 through 14 are to be answered SOLELY on the basis of the following passage.

Mental disorders are found in a fairly large number of the inmates in correctional institutions. There are no exact figures as to the number of inmates who are mentally disturbed—partly because it is hard to draw a precise line between *mental disturbance* and *normality*—but experts find that somewhere between 15% and 25% of inmates are suffering from disorders that are obvious enough to show up in routine psychiatric examinations. Society has not yet really come to grips with the problem of what to do with mentally disturbed offenders. There is not enough money available to set up treatment programs for all the people identified as mentally disturbed; and there would probably not be enough qualified psychiatric personnel available to run such programs even if they could be set up. Most mentally disturbed offenders are, therefore, left to serve out their time in correctional institutions, and the burden of dealing with them falls on correction officers. This means that a correction officer must be sensitive enough to human behavior to know when he is dealing with a person who is not mentally normal, and that the officer must be imaginative enough to be able to sense how an abnormal individual might react under certain circumstances.

10. According to the above passage, mentally disturbed inmates in correctional institutions   10.____
    A. are usually transferred to mental hospitals when their condition is noticed
    B. cannot be told from other inmates because tests cannot distinguish between sane people and normal people
    C. may constitute as much as 25% of the total inmate population
    D. should be regarded as no different from all the other inmates

11. The above passage says that today the job of handling mentally disturbed inmates is MAINLY up to
    A. psychiatric personnel
    B. other inmates
    C. correction officers
    D. administrative officials

11._____

12. Of the following, which is a reason given in the passage for society's failure to provide adequate treatment programs for mentally disturbed inmates?
    A. Law-abiding citizens should not have to pay for fancy treatment programs for criminals.
    B. A person who breaks the law should not expect society to give him special help.
    C. It is impossible to tell whether an inmate is mentally disturbed.
    D. There are not enough trained people to provide the kind of treatment needed.

12._____

13. The expression *abnormal individual*, as used in the last sentence of the passage, refers to an individual who is
    A. of average intelligence
    B. of superior intelligence
    C. completely normal
    D. mentally disturbed

13._____

14. The reader of the passage would MOST likely agree that
    A. correction officers should not expect mentally disturbed persons to behave the same way a normal person would behave
    B. correction officers should not report infractions of the rules committed by mentally disturbed persons
    C. mentally disturbed persons who break the law should be treated exactly the same way as anyone else
    D. mentally disturbed persons who have broken the law should not be imprisoned

14._____

Questions 15-19.

DIRECTIONS: Questions 15 through 19 are to be answered SOLELY on the basis of the following passage.

When a young boy or girl is released from one of the various facilities operated by the Division for Youth, supportive services to help the youth face community, group, and family pressures are needed as much as, if not more than, at any other time. These services are the responsibility of two units of the Division for Youth, the Aftercare Unit, which serves youths discharged from the urban homes, camps, and START Centers, and the Community Service Bureaus, which serve youths released from the division's school and center programs. To assure that supportive services for released youths are easily identifiable and accessible, the division has developed the *store-front* services center, located in the heart of those areas to which many of the youngsters are returning. The storefront concept and structure is able to coordinate more closely services to the particular needs and situation of the youths and to draw on the feeling of community participation and achievement by persuading the community to join in helping them.

15. Of the following, the BEST description of the storefront services center's relationship to neighborhood residents is that it
    A. actively encourages their participation
    B. accepts their help when offered
    C. asks neighborhood residents to develop rehabilitation programs
    D. limits participation to qualified neighborhood professional youth workers

16. On the basis of the paragraph, which of the following statements is CORRECT?
    A. Supportive services are not needed as much after a youth is released from a facility as during his stay.
    B. Storefront services centers are located near the facilities operated by the Division for Youth
    C. The Community Service Bureaus serve youths released from urban homes.
    D. Youths are given supportive services in their communities after release from facilities operated by the Division for Youth

17. Of the following, the MOST suitable title for the above paragraph would be
    A. PROBLEMS OF YOUTHS RETURNING TO SOCIETY
    B. COMMUNITY, GROUP, AND FAMILY PRESSURES ON RELEASED YOUTHS
    C. NEIGHBORHOOD SUPPORTIVE SERVICES FOR RELEASED YOUTHS
    D. A SURVEY OF FACILITIES OPERATED BY THE DIVISION FOR YOUTH

18. Which of the following characteristics of the storefront services is mentioned in the above paragraph?
    A. Cost   B. Availability   C. Size   D. Complexity

19. On the basis of the paragraph, which of the following statements about the Aftercare Unit is INCORRECT?
    It
    A. is a part of the Division for Youth
    B. serves youths released from school programs
    C. is similar in function to the Community Service Bureaus
    D. was partly responsible for the development of storefront centers

20. The intended purposes of imprisonment are to punish, to correct through fear of repeated punishment, to provide opportunity for penitence, and to protect society by isolating the criminal. In point of fact, other emotions—notably hate for and a desire for revenge against those responsible for their imprisonment—are a greater product of imprisonment than is fear.
    On the basis of this paragraph alone, the MOST accurate of the following conclusions is that
    A. a basis for further criminality is established by emotional factors resulting from previous imprisonment
    B. imprisonment will achieve its intended purpose only to the extent that it substitutes emotional reactions for logical thought

C. opportunities for penitence are made more necessary by the growth of a desire for revenge
D. society's protection is necessarily limited to the time an individual is imprisoned

21. The misconduct of juveniles is a symptom of some inner or outer disturbance, usually both. To the casual observer, his behavior may seem naughty or vicious, or both. To the delinquent himself, it has as much meaning as socially approved activity has for the well-behaved.
Misconduct, according to this statement,
    A. has meaning to the delinquent only if it carries with it strong social disapproval
    B. is resorted to in many cases as an attention-getter device to impress the casual observer
    C. may result from personal maladjustments and is meaningful to the delinquent
    D. stems from a juvenile's rejection of social approval for his normal activities

21.____

Questions 22-25.

DIRECTIONS: Questions 22 through 25 are to be answered SOLELY on the basis of the following passage.

There is controversy and misunderstanding about the proper function of juvenile courts and their probation departments. There are cries that the whole process produces delinquents rather than rehabilitates them. There are speeches by the score about *getting tough* with the kids. Another large group thinks we should be more understanding and gentle with delinquents. This distrust of the services offered can be attributed in large part to the confusion in the use of these services throughout the country.
On the one hand, the juvenile courts are tied to the criminal court system, with an obligation to decide guilt and innocence for offenses specifically stated and formally charged. On the other hand, they have the obligation to provide treatment, supervision, and guidance to youngsters in trouble, without respect to the crimes of which they are accused. These two conflicting assignments must be carried out—quite properly—in an informal, private way, which will not stigmatize a youngster during his formative years.
And, as the courts' preoccupation with the latter task has increased, the former (that of dispensing justice) has retreated, with the result that grave injustices are bound to occur.

22. The title below that BEST expresses the ideas of this passage is
    A. A PROBLEM FOR TODAY'S TEENAGERS
    B. REHABILITATING YOUTHFUL CRIMINALS
    C. FITTING THE PUNISHMENT TO THE CRIME
    D. JUSTICE FOR JUVENILE OFFENDERS

22.____

23. The author contends that public distrust of juvenile courts is PRIMARILY the result of
    A. the dual function of these courts
    B. lack of a sufficient number of probation officers
    C. injustices done by the courts
    D. the cost of keeping up the courts

24. The above passage suggests that the author
    A. is familiar with the problem
    B. is impatient with justice
    C. sides with those who favor leniency for juvenile offenders
    D. regards all offenses as equally important

25. The tone of the above passage is
    A. highly emotional
    B. highly personal
    C. optimistic
    D. calm

23.____
24.____
25.____

KEY (CORRECT ANSWERS)

1.	B	11.	C
2.	A	12.	D
3.	C	13.	D
4.	D	14.	A
5.	A	15.	A
6.	A	16.	D
7.	C	17.	C
8.	C	18.	B
9.	C	19.	B
10.	C	20.	A

21. C
22. D
23. A
24. A
25. D

PREPARING WRITTEN MATERIAL
EXAMINATION SECTION
TEST 1

Questions 1-15.

DIRECTIONS: For each of Questions 1 through 15, select from the options given below the MOST applicable choice, and mark your answer accordingly.
    A. The sentence is correct.
    B. The sentence contains a spelling error only.
    C. The sentence contains an English grammar error only.
    D. The sentence contains both a spelling error and an English grammar error.

1. He is a very dependible person whom we expect will be an asset to this division. 1.____

2. An investigator often finds it necessary to be very diplomatic when conducting an interview. 2.____

3. Accurate detail is especially important if court action results from an investigation. 3.____

4. The report was signed by him and I since we conducted the investigation jointly. 4.____

5. Upon receipt of the complaint, an inquiry was begun. 5.____

6. An employee has to organize his time so that he can handle his workload efficiantly. 6.____

7. It was not apparent that anyone was living at the address given by the client. 7.____

8. According to regulations, there is to be at least three attempts made to locate the client. 8.____

9. Neither the inmate nor the correction officer was willing to sign a formal statement. 9.____

10. It is our opinion that one of the persons interviewed were lying. 10.____

11. We interviewed both clients and departmental personel in the course of this investigation. 11.____

12. It is concievable that further research might produce additional evidence. 12.____

13. There are too many occurences of this nature to ignore. 13.____

14. We cannot accede to the candidate's request. 14.____

15. The submission of overdue reports is the reason that there was a delay in 15.____
completion of this investigation.

Questions 16-25.

DIRECTIONS: Each of Questions 16 through 25 may be classified under one of the following four categories:
A. Faulty because of incorrect grammar or sentence structure.
B. Faulty because of incorrect punctuation.
C. Faulty because of incorrect spelling.
D. Correct

Examine each sentence carefully to determine under which of the above four options it is best classified. Then, in the space at the right, write the letter preceding the option which is the BEST of the four suggested above. Each incorrect sentence contains but one type of error. Consider a sentence to be correct if it contains none of the types of errors mentioned, even though there may be other correct ways of expressing the same thought.

16. Although the department's supply of scratch pads and stationary have 16.____
diminished considerably, the allotment for our division has not been reduced.

17. You have not told us whom you wish to designate as your secretary. 17.____

18. Upon reading the minutes of the last meeting, the new proposal was taken 18.____
up for consideration.

19. Before beginning the discussion, we locked the door as a precautionery 19.____
measure.

20. The supervisor remarked, "Only those clerks, who perform routine work, 20.____
are permitted to take a rest period."

21. Not only will this duplicating machine make accurate copies, but it will also 21.____
produce a quantity of work equal to fifteen transcribing typists.

22. "Mr. Jones," said the supervisor, "we regret our inability to grant you an 22.____
extention of your leave of absence.

23. Although the employees find the work monotonous and fatigueing, they 23.____
rarely complain.

24. We completed the tabulation of the receipts on time despite the fact that 24.____
Miss Smith our fastest operator was absent for over a week.

25. The reaction of the employees who attended the meeting, as well as the reaction of those who did not attend, indicates clearly that the schedule is satisfactory to everyone concerned.

25.____

KEY (CORRECT ANSWERS)

1.	D	11.	B
2.	A	12.	B
3.	A	13.	B
4.	C	14.	A
5.	A	15.	C
6.	B	16.	A
7.	B	17.	D
8.	C	18.	A
9.	A	19.	C
10.	C	20.	B

21. A
22. C
23. C
24. B
25. D

TEST 2

Questions 1-15.

DIRECTIONS: Questions 1 through 15 consist of two sentences. Some are correct according to ordinary formal English usage. Others are incorrect because they contain errors in English usage, spelling, or punctuation. Consider a sentence correct if it contains no errors in English usage, spelling, or punctuation, even if there may be other ways of writing the sentence correctly. Mark your answer:
- A. If only sentence I is correct.
- B. If only sentence II is correct.
- C. If sentences 1 and II are correct.
- D. If neither sentence I nor II is correct.

1. I. The influence of recruitment efficiency upon administrative standards is readily apparant.
   II. Rapid and accurate thinking are an essential quality of the police officer.

2. I. The administrator of a police department is constantly confronted by the demands of subordinates for increased personnel in their respective units.
   II. Since a chief executive must work within well-defined fiscal limits, he must weigh the relative importance of various requests.

3. I. The two men whom the police arrested for a parking violation were wanted for robbery in three states.
   II. Strong executive control from the top to the bottom of the enterprise is one of the basic principals of police administration.

4. I. When he gave testimony unfavorable to the defendant loyalty seemed to mean very little.
   II. Having run off the road while passing a car, the patrolman gave the driver a traffic ticket.

5. I. The judge ruled that the defendant's conversation with his doctor was a privileged communication.
   II. The importance of our training program is widely recognized; however, fiscal difficulties limit the program's effectiveness.

6. I. Despite an increase in patrol coverage, there were less arrests for crimes against property this year.
   II. The investigators could hardly have expected greater cooperation from the public.

7. I. Neither the patrolman nor the witness could identify the defendant as the driver of the car.
   II. Each of the officers in the class received their certificates at the completion of the course.

8. I. The new commander made it clear that those kind of procedures would no longer be permitted.
    II. Giving some weight to performance records is more advisable than making promotions solely on the basis of test scores.

9. I. A deputy sheriff must ascertain whether the debtor, has any property.
    II. A good deputy sheriff does not cause histerical excitement when he executes a process.

10. I. Having learned that he has been assigned a judgment debtor, the deputy sheriff should call upon him.
    II. The deputy sheriff may seize and remove property without requiring a bond.

11. I. If legal procedures are not observed, the resulting contract is not enforseable.
    II. If the directions from the creditor's attorney are not in writing, the deputy sheriff should request a letter of instructions from the attorney.

12. I. The deputy sheriff may confer with the defendant and enter this defendants' place of business.
    II. A deputy sheriff must ascertain from the creditor's attorney whether the debtor has any property against which he may proceede.

13. I. The sheriff has a right to do whatever is necessary for the purpose of executing the order of the court.
    II. The written order of the court gives the sheriff general authority and he is governed in his acts by a very simple principal.

14. I. Either the patrolman or his sergeant are always ready to help the public.
    II. The sergeant asked the patrolman when he would finish the report.

15. I. The injured man could not hardly talk.
    II. Every officer had ought to had in their reports on time.

Questions 16-26.

DIRECTIONS: For each of the sentences given below, numbered 16 through 25, select from the following choices the MOST correct choice and print your choice in the space at the right. Select as your answer:
    A. If the statement contains an unnecessary word or expression
    B. If the statement contains a slang term or expression ordinarily not acceptable in government report writing.
    C. If the statement contains an old-fashioned word or expression, where a concrete, plain term would be more useful.
    D. If the statement contains no major faults.

16. Every one of us should try harder.

17. Yours of the first instant has been received.

18. We will have to do a real snow job on him.   18.____
19. I shall contact him next Thursday.   19.____
20. None of us were invited to the meeting with the community. 20.____
21. We got this here job to do.   21.____
22. She could not help but see the mistake in the checkbook.   22.____
23. Don't bug the Director about the report.   23.____
24. I beg to inform you that your letter has been received.   24.____
25. This project is all screwed up.   25.____

KEY (CORRECT ANSWERS)

1.	D	11.	B
2.	C	12.	D
3.	A	13.	A
4.	D	14.	D
5.	B	15.	D
6.	B	16.	D
7.	A	17.	C
8.	D	18.	B
9.	D	19.	D
10.	C	20.	D

21.	B
22.	D
23.	B
24.	C
25.	B

TEST 3

DIRECTIONS: Questions 1 through 25 are sentences taken from reports. Some are correct according to ordinary English usage. Others are incorrect because they contain errors in English usage, spelling, or punctuation. Consider a sentence correct if it contains no errors in English usage, spelling, or punctuation, even if there may be other ways of writing the sentence correctly. Mark your answer:
- A. If only sentence I is correct
- B. If only sentence II is correct
- C. If sentences I and II are correct
- D. If neither sentence I nor II is correct

1.
   I. The Neighborhood Police Team Commander and Team Patrolmen are encouraged to give to the public the widest possible verbal and written disemination of information regarding the existence and purposes of the program.
   II. The police must be vitally interelated with every segment of the public they serve.

   1.____

2.
   I. If social gambling, prostitution, and other vices are to be prohibited, the law makers should provide the manpower and method for enforcement.
   II. In addition to checking on possible crime locations such as hallways, roofs yards and other similar locations, Team Patrolmen are encouraged to make known their presence to members of the community.

   2.____

3.
   I. The Neighborhood Police Team Commander is authorized to secure, the cooperation of local publications, as well as public and private agencies, to further the goals of the program.
   II. Recruitment from social minorities is essential to effective police work among minorities and meaningful relations with them.

   3.____

4.
   I. The Neighborhood Police Team Commander and his men have the responsibility for providing patrol service within the sector territory on a twenty-four hour basis.
   II. While the patrolman was walking his beat at midnight he noticed that the clothing stores' door was partly open.

   4.____

5.
   I. Authority is granted to the Neighborhood Police Team to device tactics for coping with the crime in the sector.
   II. Before leaving the scene of the accident, the patrolman drew a map showing the positions of the automobiles and indicated the time of the accident as 10 M. in the morning.

   5.____

6.
   I. The Neighborhood Police Team Commander and his men must be kept apprised of conditions effecting their sector.
   II. Clear, continuous communication with every segment of the public served based on the realization of mutual need and founded on trust and confidence is the basis for effective law enforcement.

   6.____

7.   I. The irony is that the police are blamed for the laws they enforce when they are doing their duty.
     II. The Neighborhood Police Team Commander is authorized to prepare and distribute literature with pertinent information telling the public whom to contact for assistance.

7.____

8.   I. The day is not far distant when major parts of the entire police compliment will need extensive college training or degrees.
     II. Although driving under the influence of alcohol is a specific charge in making arrests, drunkenness is basically a health and social problem.

8.____

9.   I. If a deputy sheriff finds that property he has to attach is located on a ship, he should notify his supervisor.
     II. Any contract that tends to interfere with the administration of justice is illegal.

9.____

10.   I. A mandate or official order of the court to the sheriff or other officer directs it to take into possession property of the judgment debtor.
     II. Tenancies from month-to-month, week-to-week, and sometimes year-to-year are termenable.

10.____

11.   I. A civil arrest is an arrest pursuant to an order issued by a court in civil litigation.
     II. In a criminal arrest, a defendant is arrested for a crime he is alleged to have committed.

11.____

12.   I. Having taken a defendant into custody, there is a complete restraint of personal liberty.
     II. Actual force is unnecessary when a deputy sheriff makes an arrest.

12.____

13.   I. When a husband breaches a separation agreement by failing to supply to the wife the amount of money to be paid to her periodically under the agreement, the same legal steps may be taken to enforce his compliance as in any other breach of contract.
     II. Having obtained the writ of attachment, the plaintiff is then in the advantageous position of selling the very property that has been held for him by the sheriff while he was obtaining a judgment.

13.____

14.   I. Being locked in his desk, the investigator felt sure that the records would be safe.
     II. The reason why the witness changed his statement was because he had been threatened.

14.____

15.   I. The investigation had just began then an important witness disappeared.
     II. The check that had been missing was located and returned to its owner, Harry Morgan, a resident of Suffolk County, New York.

15.____

16. I. A supervisor will find that the establishment of standard procedures enables his staff to work more efficiently.
    II. An investigator hadn't ought to give any recommendations in his report if he is in doubt.

17. I. Neither the investigator nor his supervisor is ready to interview the witness.
    II. Interviewing has been and always will be an important asset in investigation.

18. I. One of the investigator's reports has been forwarded to the wrong person.
    II. The investigator stated that he was not familiar with those kind of cases.

19. I. Approaching the victim of the assault, two large bruises were noticed by me.
    II. The prisoner was arrested for assault, resisting arrest, and use of a deadly weapon.

20. I. A copy of the orders, which had been prepared by the captain, was given to each patrolman.
    II. It's always necessary to inform an arrested person of his constitutional rights before asking him any questions.

21. I. To prevent further bleeding, I applied a tourniquet to the wound.
    II. John Rano a senior officer was on duty at the time of the accident.

22. I. Limiting the term "property" to tangible property, in the criminal mischief setting, accords with prior case law holding that only tangible property came within the purview of the offense of malicious mischief.
    II. Thus, a person who intentionally destroys the property of another, but under an honest belief that he has title to such property, cannot be convicted of criminal mischief under the Revised Penal Law.

23. I. Very early in it's history, New York enacted statutes from time to time punishing, either as a felony or as a misdemeanor, malicious injuries to various kinds of property: piers, boos, dams, bridges, etc.
    II. The application of the statute is necessarily restricted to trespassory takings with larcenous intent: namely with intent permanently or virtually permanently to "appropriate" property or "deprive" the owner of its use.

24. I. Since the former Penal Law did not define the instruments of forgery in a general fashion, its crime of forgery was held to be narrower than the common law offense in this respect and to embrace only those instruments explicitly specified in the substantive provisions.
    II. After entering the barn through an open door for the purpose of stealing, it was closed by the defendants.

25. I. The use of fire or explosives to destroy tangible property is proscribed by the criminal mischief provisions of the Revised Penal Law.
    II. The defendant's taking of a taxicab for the immediate purpose of affecting his escape did not constitute grand larceny.

25.____

KEY (CORRECT ANSWERS)

1.	D	11.	C
2.	D	12.	B
3.	B	13.	C
4.	A	14.	D
5.	D	15.	B
6.	D	16.	A
7.	C	17.	C
8.	D	18.	A
9.	C	19.	B
10.	D	20.	C

21.	A
22.	C
23.	B
24.	A
25.	A

TEST 4

Questions 1-4.

DIRECTIONS: Each of the two sentences in Questions 1 through 4 may be correct or may contain errors in punctuation, capitalization, or grammar. Mark your answer:
- A. If there is an error only in sentence I
- B. If there is an error only in sentence II
- C. If there is an error in both sentences I and II
- D. If both sentences are correct.

1. I. It is very annoying to have a pencil sharpener, which is not in working order.
   II. Patrolman Blake checked the door of Joe's Restaurant and found that the lock has been jammed.

   1.____

2. I. When you are studying a good textbook is important.
   II. He said he would divide the money equally between you and me.

   2.____

3. I. Since he went on the city council a year ago, one of his primary concerns has been safety in the streets.
   II. After waiting in the doorway for about 15 minutes, a black sedan appeared.

   3.____

Questions 4-8.

DIRECTIONS: Each of the sentences in Questions 4 through 8 may be classified under one of the following four categories:
- A. Faulty because of incorrect grammar
- B. Faulty because of incorrect punctuation
- C. Faulty because of incorrect capitalization or incorrect spelling
- D. Correct

Examine each sentence carefully to determine under which of the above four options it is BEST classified. Then, in the space at the right, print the capitalized letter preceding the option which is the BEST of the four suggested above. Each faulty sentence contains but one type of error. Consider a sentence to be correct if it contains none of the types of errors mentioned, even though there may be other correct ways of expressing the same thought.

4. They told both he and I that the prisoner had escaped. 4.____

5. Any superior officer, who, disregards the just complaints of his subordinates, is remiss in the performance of his duty. 5.____

6. Only those members of the national organization who resided in the Middle west attended the conference in Chicago. 6.____

7. We told him to give the investigation assignment to whoever was available. 7.____

8. Please do not disappoint and embarass us by not appearing in court. 8.____

Questions 9-13

DIRECTIONS: Each of Questions 9 through 13 consists of three sentences lettered A, B, and C. In each of these questions, one of the sentences may contain an error in grammar, sentence structure, or punctuation, or all three sentences may be correct. If one of the sentence in a question contains an error in grammar, sentence structure, or punctuation, print in the space at the right the capital letter preceding the sentence which contains the error. If all three sentences are correct, print the letter D.

9. A. Mr. Smith appears to be less competent than I in performing these duties.
    B. The supervisor spoke to the employee, who had made the error, but did not reprimand him.
    C. When he found the book lying on the table, he immediately notified the owner.

    9.____

10. A. Being locked in the desk, we were certain that the papers would not be taken.
    B. It wasn't I who dictated the telegram; I believe it was Eleanor.
    C. You should interview whoever comes to the office today.

    10.____

11. A. The clerk was instructed to set the machine on the table before summoning the manager.
    B. He said that he was not familiar with those kind of activities.
    C. A box of pencils, in addition to erasers and blotters, was included in the shipment of supplies.

    11.____

12. A. The supervisor remarked, "Assigning an employee to the proper type of work is not always easy."
    B. The employer found that each of the applicants were qualified to perform the duties of the position.
    C. Any competent student is permitted to take this course if he obtains the consent of the instructor.

    12.____

13. A. The prize was awarded to the employee whom the judges believed to be most deserving.
    B. Since the instructor believes his book is the better of the two, he is recommending it for use in the school.
    C. It was obvious to the employees that the completion of the task by the scheduled date would require their working overtime.

    13.____

Questions 14-20.

DIRECTIONS: In answering Questions 14 through 20, choose the sentence which is BEST from the point of view of English usage suitable for a business report.

14. A. The client's receiving of public assistance checks at two different addresses were disclosed by the investigation.
    B. The investigation disclosed that the client was receiving public assistance checks at two different addresses.
    C. The client was found out by the investigation to be receiving public assistance checks at two different addresses.
    D. The client has been receiving public assistance checks at two different addresses, disclosed the investigation.

14.____

15. A. The investigation of complaints are usually handled by this unit, which deals with internal security problems in the department.
    B. This unit deals with internal security problems in the department usually investigating complaints.
    C. Investigating complaints is this unit's job, being that it handles internal security problems in the department.
    D. This unit deals with internal security problems in the department and usually investigates complaints.

15.____

16. A. The delay in completing this investigation was caused by difficulty in obtaining the required documents from the candidate.
    B. Because of difficulty in obtaining the required documents from the candidate is the reason that there was a delay in completing this investigation.
    C. Having had difficulty in obtaining the required documents from the candidate, there was a delay in completing this investigation.
    D. Difficulty in obtaining the required documents from the candidate had the affect of delaying the completion of this investigation.

16.____

17. A. This report, together with documents supporting our recommendation, are being submitted for your approval.
    B. Documents supporting our recommendation is being submitted with the report for your approval.
    C. This report, together with documents supporting our recommendation, is being submitted for your approval.
    D. The report and documents supporting our recommendation is being submitted for your approval.

17.____

18. A. The chairman himself, rather than his aides, has reviewed the report.
    B. The chairman himself, rather than his aides, have reviewed the report.
    C. The chairmen, not the aide, has reviewed the report.
    D. The aide, not the chairmen, have reviewed the report.

18.____

19. A. Various proposals were submitted but the decision is not been made.
    B. Various proposals has been submitted but the decision has not been made.
    C. Various proposals were submitted but the decision is not been made.
    D. Various proposals have been submitted but the decision has not been made.

20. A. Everyone were rewarded for his successful attempt.
    B. They were successful in their attempts and each of them was rewarded.
    C. Each of them are rewarded for their successful attempts.
    D. The reward for their successful attempts were made to each of them.

21. The following is a paragraph from a request for departmental recognition consisting of five numbered sentences submitted to a Captain for review. These sentences may or may not have errors in spelling, grammar, and punctuation:
    (1) The officers observed the subject Mills surreptitiously remove a wallet from the woman's handbag and entered his automobile. (2) As they approached Mills, he looked in their direction and drove away. (3) The officers pursued in their car. (4) Mills executed a series of complicated manuvers to evade the pursuing officers. (5) At the corner of Broome and Elizabeth Streets, Mills stopped the car, got out, raised his hands and surrendered to the officers.
    Which one of the following BEST classifies the above with regard to spelling, grammar, and punctuation?
    A. 1, 2, and 3 are correct, but 4 and 5 have errors.
    B. 2, 3, and 5 are correct, but 1 and 4 have errors.
    C. 3, 4, and 5 are correct, but 1 and 2 have errors.
    D. 1, 2, 3, and 5 are correct, but 4 has errors.

22. The one of the following sentences which is grammatically PREFERABLE to the others is:
    A. Our engineers will go over your blueprints so that you may have no problems in construction.
    B. For a long time he had been arguing that we, not he, are to blame for the confusion.
    C. I worked on his automobile for two hours and still cannot find out what is wrong with it.
    D. Accustomed to all kinds of hardships, fatigue seldom bothers veteran policemen.

23. The MOST accurate of the following sentences is:
    A. The commissioner, as well as his deputy and various bureau heads, were present.
    B. A new organization of employers and employees have been formed.
    C. One or the other of these men have been selected.
    D. The number of pages in the book is enough to discourage a reader.

24. The MOST accurate of the following sentences is: 24.____
    A. Between you and me, I think he is the better man.
    B. He was believed to be me.
    C. Is it us that you wish to see?
    D. The winners are him and her.

___

KEY (CORRECT ANSWERS)

1.	C		11.	B
2.	A		12.	B
3.	C		13.	D
4.	A		14.	B
5.	B		15.	D
6.	C		16.	A
7.	D		17.	C
8.	C		18.	A
9.	B		19.	D
10.	A		20.	B

21. B
22. A
23. D
24. A

PREPARING WRITTEN MATERIAL
EXAMINATION SECTION
TEST 1

DIRECTIONS: Each question or incomplete statement is followed by several suggested answers or completions. Select the one that BEST answers the question or completes the statement. *PRINT THE LETTER OF THE CORRECT ANSWER IN THE SPACE AT THE RIGHT.*

1. The one of the following sentences which is LEAST acceptable from the viewpoint of correct usage is:
    A. The police thought the fugitive to be him.
    B. The criminals set a trap for whoever would fall into it.
    C. It is ten years ago since the fugitive fled from the city.
    D. The lecturer argued that criminals are usually cowards.
    E. The police removed four bucketfuls of earth from the scene of the crime.

1.____

2. The one of the following sentences which is LEAST acceptable from the viewpoint of correct usage is:
    A. The patrolman scrutinized the report with great care.
    B. Approaching the victim of the assault, two bruises were noticed by the patrolman.
    C. As soon as I had broken down the door, I stepped into the room.
    D. I observed the accused loitering near the building, which was closed at the time.
    E. The storekeeper complained that his neighbor was guilty of violating a local ordinance.

2.____

3. The one of the following sentences which is LEAST acceptable from the viewpoint of correct usage is:
    A. I realized immediately that he intended to assault the woman, so I disarmed him.
    B. It was apparent that Mr. Smith's explanation contained many inconsistencies.
    C. Despite the slippery condition of the street, he managed to stop the vehicle before injuring the child.
    D. Not a single one of them wish, despite the damage to property, to make a formal complaint.
    E. The body was found lying on the floor.

3.____

4. The one of the following sentences which contains NO error in usage is:
    A. After the robbers left, the proprietor stood tied in his chair for about two hours before help arrived.
    B. In the cellar I found the watchman's hat and coat.
    C. The persons living in adjacent apartments stated that they had heard no unusual noises.

4.____

D. Neither a knife or any firearms were found in the room.
E. Walking down the street, the shouting of the crowd indicated that something was wrong.

5. The one of the following sentences which contains NO error in usage is:
   A. The policeman lay a firm hand on the suspect's shoulder.
   B. It is true that neither strength nor agility are the most important requirement for a good patrolman.
   C. Good citizens constantly strive to do more than merely comply the restraints imposed by society.
   D. No decision was made as to whom the prize should be awarded.
   E. Twenty years is considered a severe sentence for a felony.

   5.____

6. Which of the following sentences is NOT expressed in standard English usage?
   A. The victim reached a pay-phone booth and manages to call police headquarters.
   B. By the time the call was received, the assailant had left the scene.
   C. The victim has been a respected member of the community for the past eleven years.
   D. Although the lighting was bad and the shadows were deep, the storekeeper caught sight of the attacker.
   E. Additional street lights have since been installed, and the patrols have been strengthened.

   5.____

7. Which of the following sentences is NOT expressed in standard English usage?
   A. The judge upheld the attorney's right to question the witness about the missing glove.
   B. To be absolutely fair to all parties is the jury's chief responsibility.
   C. Having finished the report, a loud noise in the next room startled the sergeant.
   D. The witness obviously enjoyed having played a part in the proceedings.
   E. The sergeant planned to assign the case to whoever arrived first.

   7.____

8. In which of the following sentences is a word misused?
   A. As a matter of principle, the captain insisted that the suspect's partner be brought for questioning.
   B. The principle suspect had been detained at the station house for most of the day.
   C. The principal in the crime had no previous criminal record, but his closest associate had been convicted of felonies on two occasions.
   D. The interest payments had been made promptly, but the firm had been drawing upon the principal for these payments.
   E. The accused insisted that his high school principal would furnish him a character reference.

   8.____

9. Which of the following statements is ambiguous? 9.____
   A. Mr. Sullivan explained why Mr. Johnson had been dismissed from his job.
   B. The storekeeper told the patrolman he had made a mistake.
   C. After waiting three hours, the patients in the doctor's office were sent home.
   D. The janitor's duties were to maintain the building in good shape and to answer tenants' complaints.
   E. The speed limit should, in my opinion, be raised to sixty miles an hour on that stretch of road.

10. In which of the following is the punctuation or capitalization faulty? 10.____
    A. The accident occurred at an intersection in the Kew Gardens section of Queens, near the bus stop.
    B. The sedan, not the convertible, was struck in the side.
    C. Before any of the patrolmen had left the police car received an important message from headquarters.
    D. The dog that had been stolen was returned to his master, John Dempsey, who lived in East Village.
    E. The letter had been sent to 12 Hillside Terrace, Rutland, Vermont 05702.

Questions 11-25.

DIRECTIONS: Questions 11 through 25 are to be answered in accordance with correct English usage; that is, standard English rather than nonstandard or substandard. Nonstandard and substandard English includes words or expressions usually classified as slang, dialect, illiterate, etc., which are not generally accepted as correct in current written communication. Standard English also requires clarity, proper punctuation and capitalization and appropriate use of words. Write the letter of the sentence NOT expressed in standard English usage in the space at the right.

11. A. There were three witnesses to the accident. 11.____
    B. At least three witnesses were found to testify for the plaintiff.
    C. Three of the witnesses who took the stand was uncertain about the defendant's competence to drive.
    D. Only three witnesses came forward to testify for the plaintiff.
    E. The three witnesses to the accident were pedestrians.

12. A. The driver had obviously drunk too many martinis before leaving for home. 12.____
    B. The boy who drowned had swum in these same waters many times before.
    C. The petty thief had stolen a bicycle from a private driveway before he was apprehended.
    D. The detectives had brung in the heroin shipment they intercepted.
    E. The passengers had never ridden in a converted bus before.

13. A. Between you and me, the new platoon plan sounds like a good idea.
    B. Money from an aunt's estate was left to his wife and he.
    C. He and I were assigned to the same patrol for the first time in two months.
    D. Either you or he should check the front door of that store.
    E. The captain himself was not sure of the witness's reliability.

14. A. The alarm had scarcely begun to ring when the explosion occurred.
    B. Before the firemen arrived at the scene, the second story had been destroyed.
    C. Because of the dense smoke and heat, the firemen could hardly approach the now-blazing structure.
    D. According to the patrolman's report, there wasn't nobody in the store when the explosion occurred.
    E. The sergeant's suggestion was not at all unsound, but no one agreed with him.

15. A. The driver and the passenger they were both found to be intoxicated.
    B. The driver and the passenger talked slowly and not too clearly.
    C. Neither the driver nor his passengers were able to give a coherent account of the accident.
    D. In a corner of the room sat the passenger, quietly dozing.
    E. the driver finally told a strange and unbelievable story, which the passenger contradicted.

16. A. Under the circumstances I decided not to continue my examination of the premises.
    B. There are many difficulties now not comparable with those existing in 1960.
    C. Friends of the accused were heard to announce that the witness had better been away on the day of the trial.
    D. The two criminals escaped in the confusion that followed the explosion.
    E. The aged man was struck by the considerateness of the patrolman's offer.

17. A. An assemblage of miscellaneous weapons lay on the table.
    B. Ample opportunities were given to the defendant to obtain counsel.
    C. The speaker often alluded to his past experience with youthful offenders in the armed forces.
    D. The sudden appearance of the truck aroused my suspicions.
    E. Her studying had a good affect on her grades in high school.

18. A. He sat down in the theater and began to watch the movie.
    B. The girl had ridden horses since she was four years old.
    C. Application was made on behalf of the prosecutor to cite the witness for contempt.
    D. The bank robber, with his two accomplices, were caught in the act.
    E. His story is simply not credible.

19. A. The angry boy said that he did not like those kind of friends.
    B. The merchant's financial condition was so precarious that he felt he must avail himself of any offer of assistance.
    C. He is apt to promise more than he can perform.
    D. Looking at the messy kitchen, the housewife felt like crying.
    E. A clerk was left in charge of the stolen property.

19.____

20. A. His wounds were aggravated by prolonged exposure to sub-freezing temperatures.
    B. The prosecutor remarked that the witness was not averse to changing his story each time he was interviewed.
    C. The crime pattern indicated that the burglars were adapt in the handling of explosives.
    D. His rigid adherence to a fixed plan brought him into renewed conflict with his subordinates.
    E. He had anticipated that the sentence would be delivered by noon.

20.____

21. A. The whole arraignment procedure is badly in need of revision.
    B. After his glasses were broken in the fight, he would of gone to the optometrist if he could.
    C. Neither Tom nor Jack brought his lunch to work.
    D. He stood aside until the quarrel was over.
    E. A statement in the psychiatrist's report disclosed that the probationer vowed to have his revenge.

21.____

22. A. His fiery and intemperate speech to the striking employees fatally affected any chance of a future reconciliation.
    B. The wording of the statute has been variously construed.
    C. The defendant's attorney, speaking in the courtroom, called the official a demagogue who contempuously disregarded the judge's orders.
    D. The baseball game is likely to be the most exciting one this year.
    E. The mother divided the cookies among her two children.

22.____

23. A. There was only a bed and a dresser in the dingy room.
    B. John was one of the few students that have protested the new rule.
    C. It cannot be argued that the child's testimony is negligible; it is, on the contrary, of the greatest importance.
    D. The basic criterion for clearance was so general that officials resolved any doubts in favor of dismissal.
    E. Having just returned from a long vacation, the officer found the city unbearably hot.

23.____

24. A. The librarian ought to give more help to small children.
    B. The small boy was criticized by the teacher because he often wrote careless.
    C. It was generally doubted whether the women would permit the use of her apartment for intelligence operations.
    D. The probationer acts differently every time the officer visits him.
    E. Each of the newly appointed officers has 12 years of service.

24.____

25. A. The North is the most industrialized region in the country.
    B. L. Patrick Gray 3d, the bureau's acting director, stated that, while "rehabilitation is fine" for some convicted criminals, "it is a useless gesture for those who resist every such effort."
    C. Careless driving, faulty mechanism, narrow or badly kept roads all play their part in causing accidents.
    D. The childrens' books were left in the bus.
    E. It was a matter of internal security; consequently, he felt no inclination to rescind his previous order.

25.____

KEY (CORRECT ANSWERS)

1.	C	11.	C
2.	B	12.	D
3.	D	13.	B
4.	C	14.	D
5.	E	15.	A
6.	A	16.	C
7.	C	17.	E
8.	B	18.	D
9.	B	19.	A
10.	C	20.	C

21.	B
22.	E
23.	B
24.	B
25.	D

TEST 2

DIRECTIONS: Each question or incomplete statement is followed by several suggested answers or completions. Select the one that BEST answers the question or completes the statement. *PRINT THE LETTER OF THE CORRECT ANSWER IN THE SPACE AT THE RIGHT.*

Questions 1-6.

DIRECTIONS: Each of Questions 1 through 6 consists of a statement which contains a word (one of those underlined) that is either incorrectly used because it is not in keeping with the meaning the quotation is evidently intended to convey, or is misspelled. There is only one INCORRECT word in each quotation. Of the four underlined words, determine if the first one should be replaced by the word lettered A, the second replaced by the word lettered B, the third replaced by the word lettered C, or the fourth replaced by the word lettered D.

1. Whether one depends on fluorescent or artificial light or both, adequate standards should be maintained by means of systematic tests.
   A. natural   B. safeguards   C. established   D. routine

1.____

2. A police officer has to be prepared to assume his knowledge as a social scientist in the community.
   A. forced   B. role   C. philosopher   D. street

2.____

3. It is practically impossible to indicate whether a sentence is too long simply by measuring its length.
   A. almost   B. tell   C. very   D. guessing

3.____

4. Strong leaders are required to organize a community for delinquency prevention and for dissemination of organized crime and drug addiction.
   A. tactics   B. important   C. control   D. meetings

4.____

5. The demonstrators who were taken to the Criminal Courts building in Manhattan (because it was large enough to accommodate them), contended that the arrests were unwarranted.
   A. demonstraters   B. Manhatten
   C. accomodate   D. unwarranted

5.____

6. They were guaranteed a calm atmosphere, free from harassment, which would be conducive to quiet consideration of the indictments.
   A. guarenteed   B. atmspher
   C. harassment   D. inditements

6.____

Questions 7-11.

DIRECTIONS: Each of Questions 7 through 11 consists of a statement containing four words in capital letters. One of these words in capital letters is not in keeping with the meaning which the statement is evidently intended to carry. The four words in capital letters in each statement are reprinted after the statement. Print the capital letter preceding the one of the four words which does MOST to spoil the true meaning of the statement in the space at the right.

7. Retirement and pension systems are essential not only to provide employees with with a means of support in the future, but also to prevent longevity and CHARITABLE considerations from UPSETTING the PROMOTIONAL opportunities RETIRED members of the career service.
   A. charitable   B. upsetting   C. promotional   D. retired

7.____

8. Within each major DIVISION in a properly set up public or private organization, provision is made so that each NECESSARY activity is CARED for and lines of authority and responsibility are clear-cut and INFINITE.
   A. division   B. necessary   C. cared   D. infinite

8.____

9. In public service, the scale of salaries paid must be INCIDENTAL to the services rendered, with due CONSIDERATION for the attraction of the desired MANPOWER and for the maintenance of a standard of living COMMENSURATE with the work to be performed.
   A. incidental   B. consideration
   C. manpower   D. commensurate

9.____

10. An understanding of the AIMS of an organization by the staff will AID greatly in increasing the DEMAND of the correspondence work of the office, and will to a large extent DETERMINE the nature of the correspondence.
    A. aims   B. aid   C. demand   D. determine

10.____

11. BECAUSE the Civil Service Commission strongly feels that the MERIT system is a key factor in the MAINTENANCE of democratic government, it has adopted as one of its major DEFENSES the progressive democratization of its own procedures in dealing with candidates for positions in the public service.
    A. Because   B. merit   C. maintenance   D. defenses

11.____

Questions 12-14.

DIRECTIONS: Questions 12 through 14 consist of one sentence each. Each sentence contains an incorrectly used word. First, decide which is the incorrectly used word. Then, from among the options given, decide which word, when substituted for the incorrectly used word, makes the meaning of the sentence clear.
EXAMPLE:
The U.S. national income exhibits a pattern of long term deflection.
   A. reflection   B. subjection   C. rejoicing   D. growth

The word *deflection* in the sentence does not convey the meaning the sentence evidently intended to convey. The word *growth* (Answer D), when substituted for the word *deflection*, makes the meaning of the sentence clear. Accordingly, the answer to the question is D.

12. The study commissioned by the joint committee fell compassionately short of the mark and would have to be redone.
    A. successfully
    B. insignificantly
    C. experimentally
    D. woefully

13. He will not idly exploit any violation of the provisions of the order.
    A. tolerate   B. refuse   C. construe   D. guard

14. The defendant refused to be virile and bitterly protested service.
    A. irked   B. feasible   C. docile   D. credible

Questions 15-25.

DIRECTIONS: Questions 15 through 25 consist of short paragraphs. Each paragraph contains one word which is INCORRECTLY used because it is NOT in keeping with the meaning of the paragraph. Find the word in each paragraph which is INCORRECTLY used and then select as the answer the suggested word which should be substituted for the incorrectly used word.

SAMPLE QUESTION:
In determining who is to do the work in your unit, you will have to decide just who does what from day to day. One of your lowest responsibilities is to assign work so that everybody gets a fair share and that everyone can do his part well.
    A. new   B. old   C. important   D. performance

EXPLANATION:
The word which is NOT in keeping with the meaning of the paragraph is *lowest*. This is the INCORRECTLY used word. The suggested word *important* would be in keeping with the meaning of the paragraph and should be substituted for *lowest*. Therefore, the CORRECT answer is choice C.

15. If really good practice in the elimination of preventable injuries is to be achieved and held in any establishment, top management must refuse full and definite responsibility and must apply a good share of its attention to the task.
    A. accept   B. avoidable   C. duties   D. problem

16. Recording the human face for identification is by no means the only service performed by the camera in the field of investigation. When the trial of any issue takes place, a word picture is sought to be distorted to the court of incidents, occurrences, or events which are in dispute.
    A. appeals   B. description   C. portrayed   D. deranged

17. In the collection of physical evidence, it cannot be emphasized too strongly that a haphazard systematic search at the scene of the crime is vital. Nothing must be overlooked. Often the only leads in a case will come from the results of this search.
    A. important   B. investigation
    C. proof   D. thorough

18. If an investigator has reason to suspect that the witness is mentally stable, or a habitual drunkard, he should leave no stone unturned in his investigation to determine if the witness was under the influence of liquor or drugs, or was mentally unbalanced either at the time of the occurrence to which he testified or at the time of the trial.
    A. accused   B. clue   C. deranged   D. question

19. The use of records is a valuable step in crime investigation and is the main reason every department should maintain accurate reports. Crimes are not committed through the use of departmental records alone but from the use of all records, of almost every type, wherever they may be found and whenever they give any incidental information regarding the criminal.
    A. accidental   B. necessary   C. reported   D. solved

20. In the years since passage of the Harrison Narcotic Act of 1914, making the possession of opium amphetamines illegal in most circumstances, drug use has become a subject of considerable scientific interest and investigation. There is at present a voluminous literature on drug use of various kinds.
    A. ingestion   B. derivatives   C. addiction   D. opiates

21. Of course, the fact that criminal laws are extremely patterned in definition does not mean that the majority of persons who violate them are dealt with as criminals. Quite the contrary, for a great many forbidden acts are voluntarily engaged in within situations of privacy and go unobserved and unreported.
    A. symbolic   B. casual   C. scientific   D. broad-gauged

22. The most punitive way to study punishment is to focus attention on the pattern of punitive action: to study how a penalty is applied, too study what is done to or taken from an offender.
    A. characteristic   B. degrading   C. objective   D. distinguished

23. The most common forms of punishment in times past have been death, physical torture, mutilation, branding, public humiliation, fines, forfeits of property, banishment, transportation, and imprisonment. Although this list is by no means differentiated, practically every form of punishment has had several variations and applications.
    A. specific   B. simple   C. exhaustive   D. characteristic

24. There is another important line of inference between ordinary and professional criminals, and that is the source from which they are recruited. The professional criminal seems to be drawn from legitimate employment and, in many instances, from parallel vocations or pursuits. 24.____
   A. demarcation   B. justification   C. superiority   D. reference

25. He took the position that the success of the program was insidious on getting additional revenue. 25.____
   A. reputed   B. contingent   C. failure   D. indeterminate

KEY (CORRECT ANSWERS)

1.	A	11.	D
2.	B	12.	D
3.	B	13.	A
4.	C	14.	C
5.	D	15.	A
6.	C	16.	C
7.	D	17.	D
8.	D	18.	C
9.	A	19.	D
10.	C	20.	B

21.	D
22.	C
23.	C
24.	A
25.	B

TEST 3

DIRECTIONS: Each question or incomplete statement is followed by several suggested answers or completions. Select the one that BEST answers the question or completes the statement. *PRINT THE LETTER OF THE CORRECT ANSWER IN THE SPACE AT THE RIGHT.*

Questions 1-5.

DIRECTIONS: Questions 1 through 5 are to be answered on the basis of the following.

You are a supervising officer in an investigative unit. Earlier in the day, you directed Detectives Tom Dixon and Sal Mayo to investigate a reported assault and robbery in a liquor store within your area of jurisdiction.

Detective Dixon has submitted to you a preliminary investigative report containing the following information:

- At 1630 hours on 2/20, arrived at Joe's Liquor Store at 350 SW Avenue with Detective Mayo to investigate A & R.
- At store interviewed Rob Ladd, store manager, who stated that he and Joe Brown (store owner) had been stuck up about ten minutes prior to our arrival.
- Ladd described the robbers as male whites in their late teens or early twenties. Further stated that one of the robbers displayed what appeared to be an automatic pistol as he entered the store, and said, *Give us the money or we'll kill you.* Ladd stated that Brown then reached under the counter where he kept a loaded .38 caliber pistol. Several shots followed, and Ladd threw himself to the floor.
- The robbers fled, and Ladd didn't know if any money had been taken.
- At this point, Ladd realized that Brown was unconscious on the floor and bleeding from a head wound.
- Ambulance called by Ladd, and Brown was removed by same to General Hospital.
- Personally interviewed John White, 382 Dartmouth Place, who stated he was inside store at the time of occurrence. White states that he hid behind a wine display upon hearing someone say, *Give us the money.* He then heard shots and saw two young men run from the store to a yellow car parked at the curb. White was unable to further describe auto. States the taller of the two men drove the car away while the other sat on passenger side in front.
- Recovered three spent .38 caliber bullets from premises and delivered them to Crime Lab.
- To General Hospital at 1800 hours but unable to interview Brown, who was under sedation and suffering from shock and a laceration of the head.
- Alarm #12487 transmitted for car and occupants.
- Case Active.

Based solely on the contents of the preliminary investigation submitted by Detective Dixon, select one sentence from the following groups of sentences which is MOST accurate and is grammatically correct.

1. A. Both robbers were armed.
   B. Each of the robbers were described as a male white.
   C. Neither robber was armed.
   D. Mr. Ladd stated that one of the robbers was armed.

   1.____

2. A. Mr. Brown fired three shots from his revolver.
   B. Mr. Brown was shot in the head by one of the robbers.
   C. Mr. Brown suffered a gunshot wound of the head during the course of the robbery.
   D. Mr. Brown was taken to General Hospital by ambulance.

   2.____

3. A. Shots were fired after one of the robbers said, *Give us the money or we'll kill you.*
   B. After one of the robbers demanded the money from Mr. Brown, he fired a shot.
   C. The preliminary investigation indicated that although Mr. Brown did not have a license for the gun, he was justified in using deadly physical force.
   D. Mr. Brown was interviewed at General Hospital.

   3.____

4. A. Each of the witnesses were customers in the store at the time of occurrence.
   B. Neither of the witnesses interviewed was the owner of the liquor store.
   C. Neither of the witnesses interviewed were the owner of the store.
   D. Neither of the witnesses was employed by Mr. Brown.

   4.____

5. A. Mr. Brown arrived at General Hospital at about 5:00 P.M.
   B. Neither of the robbers was injured during the robbery.
   C. The robbery occurred at 3:30 P.M. on February 10.
   D. One of the witnesses called the ambulance.

   5.____

Questions 6-10.

DIRECTIONS: Each of Questions 6 through 10 consists of information given in outline form and four sentences labeled A, B, C, and D. For each question, choose the one sentence which CORRECTLY expresses the information given in outline form and which also displays PROPER English usage.

6. Client's Name: Joanna Jones
   Number of Children: 3
   Client's Income: None
   Client's Marital Status: Single

   6.____

   A. Joanna Jones is an unmarried client with three children who have no income.
   B. Joanna Jones, who is single and has no income, a client she has three children.
   C. Joanna Jones, whose three children are clients, is single and has no income.
   D. Joanna Jones, who has three children, is an unmarried client with no income.

7. Client's Name: Bertha Smith
   Number of Children: 2
   Client's Rent: $1050 per month
   Number of Rooms: 4

   A. Bertha Smith, a client, pays $1050 per month for her four rooms with two children.
   B. Client Bertha Smith has two children and pays $1050 per month for four rooms.
   C. Client Bertha Smith is paying $1050 per month for two children with four rooms.
   D. For four rooms and two children client Bertha Smith pays $1050 per month.

7._____

8. Name of Employee: Cynthia Dawes
   Number of Cases Assigned: 9
   Date Cases were Assigned: 12/16
   Number of Assigned Cases Completed: 8

   A. On December 16, employee Cynthia Dawes was assigned nine cases; she has completed eight of these cases.
   B. Cynthia Dawes, employee on December 16, assigned nine cases, completed eight.
   C. Being employed on December 16, Cynthia Dawes completed eight of nine assigned cases.
   D. Employee Cynthia Dawes, she was assigned nine cases and completed eight, on December 16.

8._____

9. Place of Audit: Broadway Center
   Names of Auditors: Paul Cahn, Raymond Perez
   Date of Audit: 11/20
   Number of Cases Audited: 41

   A. On November 20, at the Broadway Center 41 cases was audited by auditors Paul Cahn and Raymond Perez.
   B. Auditors Raymond Perez and Paul Cahn has audited 41 cases at the Broadway Center on November 20.
   C. At the Broadway Center, on November 20, auditors Paul Cahn and Raymond Perez audited 41 cases.
   D. Auditors Paul Cahn and Raymond Perez at the Broadway Center, on November 20, is auditing 41 cases.

9._____

10. Name of Client: Barbra Levine
    Client's Monthly Income: $2100
    Client's Monthly Expenses: $4520

    A. Barbra Levine is a client, her monthly income is $2100 and her monthly expenses is $4520.
    B. Barbra Levine's monthly income is $2100 and she is a client, with whose monthly expenses are $4520.

10._____

C. Barbra Levine is a client whose monthly income is $2100 and whose monthly expenses are $4520.
D. Barbra Levine, a client, is with a monthly income which is $2100 and monthly expenses which are $4520.

Questions 11-13.

DIRECTIONS: Questions 11 through 13 involve several statements of fact presented in a very simple way. These statements of fact are followed by 4 choices which attempt to incorporate all of the facts into one logical statement which is properly constructed and grammatically correct.

11. I. Mr. Brown was sweeping the sidewalk in front of his house.
    II. He was sweeping it because it was dirty.
    III. He swept the refuse into the street.
    IV. Police Officer gave him a ticket.

    Which one of the following BEST presents the information given above?
    A. Because his sidewalk was dirty, Mr. Brown received a ticket from Officer Green when he swept the refuse into the street.
    B. Police Officer Green gave Mr. Brown a ticket because his sidewalk was dirty and he swept the refuse into the street.
    C. Police Officer Green gave Mr. Brown a ticket for sweeping refuse into the street because his sidewalk was dirty.
    D. Mr. Brown, who was sweeping refuse from his dirty sidewalk into the street, was given a ticket by Police Officer Green.

12. I. Sergeant Smith radioed for help.
    II. The sergeant did so because the crowd was getting larger.
    III. It was 10:00 A.M. when he made his call.
    IV. Sergeant Smith was not in uniform at the time of occurrence.

    Which one of the following BEST presents the information given above?
    A. Sergeant Smith, although not on duty at the time, radioed for help at 10 o'clock because the crowd was getting uglier.
    B. Although not in uniform, Sergeant Smith called for help at 10:00 A.M. because the crowd was getting uglier.
    C. Sergeant Smith radioed for help at 10:00 A.M. because the crowd was getting larger.
    D. Although he was not in uniform, Sergeant Smith radioed for help at 10:00 A.M. because the crowd was getting larger.

13. I. The payroll office is open on Fridays.
    II. Paychecks are distributed from 9:00 A.M. to 12 Noon.
    III. The office is open on Fridays because that's the only day the payroll staff is available.
    IV. It is open for the specified hours in order to permit employees to cash checks at the bank during lunch hour.

The choice below which MOST clearly and accurately presents the above idea is:
- A. Because the payroll office is open on Fridays from 9:00 A.M. to 12 Noon, employees can cash their checks when the payroll staff is available.
- B. Because the payroll staff is only available on Fridays until noon, employees can cash their checks during their lunch hour.
- C. Because the payroll staff is available only on Fridays, the office is open from 9:00 A.M. to 12 Noon to allow employees to cash their checks.
- D. Because of payroll staff availability, the payroll office is open on Fridays. It is open from 9:00 A.M. to 12 Noon so that distributed paychecks can be cashed at the bank while employees are on their lunch hour.

Questions 14-16.

DIRECTIONS: In each of Questions 14 through 6, the four sentences are from a paragraph in a report. They are not in the right order. Which of the following arrangements is the BEST one?

14.
   I. An executive may answer a letter by writing his reply on the face of the letter itself instead of having a return letter typed.
   II. This procedure is efficient because it saves the executive's time, the typist's time, and saves office file space.
   III. Copying machines are used in small offices as well as large offices to save time and money in making brief replies to business letters.
   IV. A copy is made on a copy machine to go into the company files, while the original is mailed back to the sender.

   The CORRECT answer is:
   A. I, II, IV, III   B. I, IV, II, III   C. III, I, IV, II   D. III, IV, II, I

15.
   I. Most organizations favor one of the types but always include the others to a lesser degree.
   II. However, we can detect a definite trend toward greater use of symbolic control.
   III. We suggest that our local police agencies are today primarily utilizing material control.
   IV. Control can be classified into three types: physical, material, and symbolic.

   The CORRECT answer is:
   A. IV, II, III, I   B. II, I, IV, III   C. III, IV, II, I   D. IV, I, III, II

16.
   I. They can and do take advantage of ancient political and geographical boundaries, which often give them sanctuary from effective policy activity.
   II. This country is essentially a country of small police forces, each operating independently within the limits of its jurisdiction.
   III. The boundaries that define and limit police operations do not hinder the movement of criminals, of course.
   IV. The machinery of law enforcement in America is fragmented, complicated, and frequently overlapping.

The CORRECT answer is:
A. III, I, IV B. II, IV, I, III C. IV, II, III, I D. IV, III, II, I

17. Examine the following sentence, and then choose from below the words which should be inserted in the blank spaces to produce the best sentence.
The unit has exceeded _____ goals and the employees are satisfied with _____ accomplishments.
A. their, it's B. it's; it's C. its, there D. its, their

18. Examine the following sentence, and then choose from below the words which should be inserted in the blank spaces to produce the best sentence.
Research indicates that employees who _____ no opportunity for close social relationships often find their work unsatisfying, and this _____ of satisfaction often reflects itself in low production.
A. have; lack B. have; excess C. has; lack D. has; excess

19. Words in a sentence must be arranged properly to make sure that the intended meaning of the sentence is clear.
The sentence below that does NOT make sense because a clause has been separated from the word on which its meaning depends is:
A. To be a good writer, clarity is necessary.
B. To be a good writer, you must write clearly.
C. You must write clearly to be a good writer.
D. Clarity is necessary to good writing.

Questions 20-21.

DIRECTIONS: Each of Questions 20 and 21 consists of a statement which contains a word (one of those underlined) that is either incorrectly used because it is not in keeping with the meaning the quotation is evidently intended to convey, or is misspelled. There is only one INCORRECT word in each quotation. Of the four underlined words, determine if the first one should be replaced by the word lettered A, the second one replaced by the word lettered B, the third one replaced by the word lettered C, or the fourth one replaced by the word lettered D.

20. The alleged killer was occasionally permitted to excercise in the corridor.
A. alledged B. ocasionally C. permited D. exercise

21. Defense counsel stated, in affect, that their conduct was permissible under the First Amendment.
A. council B. effect C. there D. permissable

Question 22.

DIRECTIONS: Question 22 consists of one sentence. This sentence contains an incorrectly used word. First, decide which is the incorrectly used word. Then, from among the options given, decide which word, when substituted for the incorrectly used word, makes the meaning of the sentence clear.

22. As today's violence has no single cause, so its causes have no single scheme. 22.____
    A. deference   B. cure   C. flaw   D. relevance

23. In the sentence, *A man in a light-grey suit waited thirty-five minutes in the ante-room for the all-important document*, the word IMPROPERLY hyphenated is   23.____
    A. light-grey   B. thirty-five
    C. ante-room   D. all-important

24. In the sentence, *The candidate wants to file his application for preference before it is too late*, the word *before* is used as a(n)   24.____
    A. preposition   B. subordinating conjunction
    C. pronoun   D. adverb

25. In the sentence, *The perpetrators ran from the scene*, the word *from* is a   25.____
    A. preposition   B. pronoun   C. verb   D. conjunction

KEY (CORRECT ANSWERS)

1.	D		11.	D
2.	D		12.	D
3.	A		13.	D
4.	B		14.	C
5.	D		15.	D
6.	D		16.	C
7.	B		17.	D
8.	A		18.	A
9.	C		19.	A
10.	C		20.	D

21. B
22. B
23. C
24. B
25. A

PREPARING WRITTEN MATERIAL

PARAGRAPH REARRANGEMENT
COMMENTARY

The sentences that follow are in scrambled order. You are to rearrange them in proper order and indicate the letter choice containing the correct answer at the space at the right.

Each group of sentences in this section is actually a paragraph presented in scrambled order. Each sentence in the group has a place in that paragraph; no sentence is to be left out. You are to read each group of sentences and decide upon the best order in which to put the sentences so as to form a well-organized paragraph.

The questions in this section measure the ability to solve a problem when all the facts relevant to its solution are not given.

More specifically, certain positions of responsibility and authority require the employee to discover connection between events sometimes, apparently, unrelated. In order to do this, the employee will find it necessary to correctly infer that unspecified events have probably occurred or are likely to occur. This ability becomes especially important when action must be taken on incomplete information.

Accordingly, these questions require competitors to choose among several suggested alternatives, each of which presents a different sequential arrangement of the events. Competitors must choose the MOST logical of the suggested sequences.

In order to do so, they may be required to draw on general knowledge to infer missing concepts or events that are essential to sequencing the given events. Competitors should be careful to infer only what is essential to the sequence. The plausibility of the wrong alternatives will always require the inclusion of unlikely events or of additional chains of events which are NOT essential to sequencing the given events.

It's very important to remember that you are looking for the best of the four possible choices, and that the best choice of all may not even be one of the answers you're given to choose from.

There is no one right way to solve these problems. Many people have found it helpful to first write out the order of the sentences, as they would have arranged them, on their scrap paper before looking at the possible answers. If their optimum answer is there, this can save them some time. If it isn't, this method can still give insight into solving the problem. Others find it most helpful to just go through each of the possible choices, contrasting each as they go along. You should use whatever method feels comfortable and works for you.

While most of these types of questions are not that difficult, we've added a higher percentage of the difficult type, just to give you more practice. Usually there are only one or two questions on this section that contain such subtle distinctions that you're unable to answer confidently. And you then may find yourself stuck deciding between two possible choices, neither of which you're sure about.

EXAMINATION SECTION

TEST 1

DIRECTIONS: Each question consists of several sentences which can be arranged in a logical sequence. For each question, select the choice which places the numbered sentences in the MOST logical sequence. *PRINT THE LETTER OF THE CORRECT ANSWER IN THE SPACE AT THE RIGHT.*

1. I. A body was found in the woods.
    II. A man proclaimed innocence.
    III. The owner of a gun was located.
    IV. A gun was traced.
    V. The owner of a gun was questioned.
    The CORRECT answer is:
    A. IV, III, V, II, I   B. II, I, IV, III, V   C. I, IV, III, V, II
    D. I, III, V, II, IV   E. I, II, IV, III, V

    1.____

2. I. A man is in a hunting accident.
    II. A man fell down a flight of steps.
    III. A man lost his vision in one eye.
    IV. A man broke his leg.
    V. A man had to walk with a cane.
    The CORRECT answer is:
    A. II, IV, V, I, III   B. IV, V, I, III, II   C. III, I, IV, V, II
    D. I, III, V, II, IV   E. I, III, II, IV, V

    2.____

3. I. A man is offered a new job.
    II. A woman is offered a new job.
    III. A man works as a waiter.
    IV. A woman works as a waitress.
    V. A woman gives notice.
    The CORRECT answer is:
    A. IV, II, V, III, I   B. IV, II, V, I, III   C. II, IV, V, III, I
    D. III, I, IV, II, V   E. IV, III, II, V, I

    3.____

4. I. A train let the station late.
    II. A man was late for work.
    III. A man lost his job.
    IV. Many people complained because the train was late.
    V. There was a traffic jam.
    The CORRECT answer is:
    A. V, II, I, IV, III   B. V, I, IV, II, III   C. V, I, II, IV, III
    D. I, V, IV, II, III   E. II, I, IV, V, III

    4.____

5. I. The burden of proof as to each issue is determined before trial and remains upon the same party throughout the trial.
    II. The jury is at liberty to believe one witness' testimony as against a number of contradictory witnesses.
    III. In a civil case, the party bearing the burden of proof is required to prove his contention by a fair preponderance of the evidence.
    IV. However, it must be noted that a fair preponderance of evidence does not necessarily mean a greater number of witnesses.
    V. The burden of proof is the burden which rests upon one of the parties to an action to persuade the trier of the facts, generally the jury, that a proposition he asserts is true.
    VI. If the evidence is equally balanced, or if it leaves the jury in such doubt as to be unable to decide the controversy either way, judgment must be given against the party upon whom the burden of proof rests.
    The CORRECT answer is:
    A. III, II, V, IV, I, VI B. I, II, VI, V, III, IV C. III, IV, V, I, II, VI
    D. V, I, III, VI, IV, II E. I, V, III, VI, IV, II

6. I. If a parent is without assets and is unemployed, he cannot be convicted of the crime of non-support of a child.
    II. The term *sufficient ability* has been held to mean sufficient financial ability.
    III. It does not matter if his unemployment is by choice or unavoidable circumstances.
    IV. If he fails to take any steps at all, he may be liable to prosecution for endangering the welfare of a child.
    V. Under the penal law, a parent is responsible for the support of his minor child only if the parent is of *sufficient ability*.
    VI. An indigent parent may meet his obligation by borrowing money or by seeking aid under the provisions of the Social Welfare Law.
    The CORRECT answer is:
    A. VI, I, V, III, II, IV B. I, III, V, II, IV, VI C. V, II, I, III, VI, IV
    D. I, VI, IV, V, II, III E. II, V, I, III, VI, IV

7. I. Consider, for example, the case of a rabble rouser who urges a group of twenty people to go out and break the windows of a nearby factory.
    II. Therefore, the law fills the indicated gap with the crime of *inciting to riot*.
    III. A person is considered guilty of inciting to riot when he urges ten or more persons to engage in tumultuous and violent conduct of a kind likely to create public alarm.
    IV. However, if he has not obtained the cooperation of at least four people, he cannot be charged with unlawful assembly.
    V. The charge of inciting to riot was added to the law to cover types of conduct which cannot be classified as either the crime of *riot* or the crime of *unlawful assembly*.
    VI. If he acquires the acquiescence of at least four of them, he is guilty of unlawful assembly even if the project does not materialize.
    The CORRECT answer is:
    A. III, V, I, VI, IV, II B. V, I, IV, VI, II, III C. III, IV, I, V, II, VI
    D. V, I, IV, VI, III, II E. V, III, I, VI, IV, II

8. I. If, however, the rebuttal evidence presents an issue of credibility, it is for the jury to determine whether the presumption has, in fact, been destroyed.
    II. Once sufficient evidence to the contrary is introduced, the presumption disappears from the trial.
    III. The effect of a presumption is to place the burden upon the adversary to come forward with evidence to rebut the presumption.
    IV. When a presumption is overcome and ceases to exist in the case, the fact or facts which gave rise to the presumption still remain.
    V. Whether a presumption has been overcome is ordinarily a question for the court.
    VI. Such information may furnish a basis for a logical inference.
    The CORRECT answer is:
    A. IV, VI, II, V, I, III   B. III, II, V, I, IV, VI   C. V, III, VI, IV, II, I
    D. V, IV, I, II, VI, III   E. II, III, V, I, IV, VI

8.____

9. I. An executive may answer a letter by writing his reply on the face of the letter itself instead of having a return letter typed.
    II. This procedure is efficient because it saves the executive's time, the typist's time, and saves office file space.
    III. Copying machines are used in small offices as well as large offices to save time and money in making brief replies to business letters.
    IV. A copy is made on a copying machine to go into the company files, while the original is mailed back to the sender.
    The CORRECT answer is:
    A. I, II, IV, III   B. I, IV, II, III   C. III, I, IV, II   D. III, IV, II, I

9.____

10. I. Most organizations favor one of the types but always include the others to a lesser degree.
    II. However, we can detect a definite trend toward greater use of symbolic control.
    III. We suggest that our local police agencies are today primarily utilizing material control.
    IV. Control can be classified into three types: physical, material, and symbolic.
    The CORRECT answer is:
    A. IV, II, III, I   B. II, I, IV, III   C. III, IV, II, I   D. IV, I, III, II

10.____

11. I. Project residents had first claim to this use, followed by surrounding neighborhood children.
    II. By contrast, recreation space within the project's interior was found to be used more often by both groups.
    III. Studies of the use of project grounds in many cities showed grounds left open for public use were neglected and unused, both by residents and by members of the surrounding community.
    IV. Project residents had clearly laid claim to the play spaces, setting up and enforcing unwritten rules for use.
    V. Each group, by experience, found their activities easily disrupted by other groups, and their claim to the use of space for recreation difficult to enforce.

11.____

The CORRECT answer is:
A. IV, V, I, II, III
B. V, II, IV, III, I
C. I, IV, III, II, V
D. III, V, II, IV, I

12. I. They do not consider the problems correctable within the existing subsidy formula and social policy of accepting all eligible applicants regardless of social behavior.
    II. A recent survey, however, indicated that tenants believe these problems correctable by local housing authorities and management within the existing financial formula.
    III. Many of the problems and complaints concerning public housing management and design have created resentment between the tenant and the landlord.
    IV. This same survey indicated that administrators and managers do not agree with the tenants.
    The CORRECT answer is:
    A. II, I, III, IV   B. I, III, IV, II   C. III, II, IV, I   D. IV, II, I, III

13. I. In single-family residences, there is usually enough distance between tenants to prevent occupants from annoying one another.
    II. For example, a certain small percentage of tenant families has one or more members addicted to alcohol.
    III. While managers believe in the right of individuals to live as they choose, the manager becomes concerned when the pattern of living jeopardizes others' rights.
    IV. Still others turn night into day, staging lusty entertainments which carry on into the hours when most tenants are trying to sleep.
    V. In apartment buildings, however, tenants live so closely together that any misbehavior can result in unpleasant living conditions.
    VI. Other families engage in violent argument.
    The CORRECT answer is:
    A. III, II, V, IV, VI, I
    B. I, V, II, VI, IV, III
    C. II, V, IV, I, III, VI
    D. IV, II, V, VI, III, I

14. I. Congress made the commitment explicit in the Housing Act of 194, establishing as a national goal the realization of a *decent home and suitable environment for every American family*.
    II. The result has been that the goal of decent home and suitable environment is still as far distant as ever for the disadvantaged urban family.
    III. In spite of this action by Congress, federal housing programs have continued to be fragmented and grossly underfunded.
    IV. The passage of the National Housing Act signaled a few federal commitment to provide housing for the nation's citizens.
    The CORRECT answer is:
    A. I, IV, III, II   B. IV, I, III, II   C. IV, I, II, III   D. II, IV, I, III

15.
   I. The greater expense does not necessarily involve *exploitation*, but it is often perceived as exploitative and unfair by those who are aware of the price differences involved, but unaware of operating costs.
   II. Ghetto residents believe they are *exploited* by local merchants, and evidence substantiates some of these beliefs.
   III. However, stores in low-income areas were more likely to be small independents, which could not achieve the economies available to supermarket chains and were, therefore, more likely to charge higher prices, and the customers were more likely to buy smaller-sized packages which are more expensive per unit of measure.
   IV. A study conducted in one city showed that distinctly higher prices were charged for goods sold in ghetto stores in other areas.
   The CORRECT answer is:
   A. IV, II, I, III   B. IV, I, III, II   C. II, IV, III, I   D. II, III, IV, I

15.____

KEY (CORRECT ANSWERS)

1. C   6. C   11. D
2. E   7. A   12. C
3. B   8. B   13. B
4. B   9. C   14. B
5. D   10. D   15. C

EXAMINATION SECTION
TEST 1

DIRECTIONS: The sentences listed below are part of a meaningful paragraph, but they are not given in their proper order. You are to decide what would be the BEST order to put sentences to form a well-organized paragraph. Each sentence has a place in the paragraph; there are no extra sentences. *PRINT THE LETTER OF THE CORRECT ANSWER IN THE SPACE AT THE RIGHT.*

1.
   I. He came on a winter's eve.
   II. Akira came directly, breaking all tradition.
   III. He pounded on the door while a cold rain beat on the shuttered veranda, so at first Chie thought him only the wind.
   IV. Was that it?
   V. Had he followed form—had he asked his mother to speak to his father to approach a go-between—would Chie have been more receptive?
   The CORRECT answer is:
   A. II, IV, V, I, III   B. I, III, II, IV, V   C. V, IV, II, III, I   D. III, V, I, II, IV

   1.____

2.
   I. We have an understanding.
   II. Either method comes down to the same thing: a matter of parental approval.
   III. If you give your consent, I become Naomi's husband.
   IV. Please don't judge my candidacy by the unseemliness of this proposal.
   V. I ask directly because the use of a go-between takes much time.
   The CORRECT answer is:
   A. III, IV, II, V, I   B. I, V, II, III, IV   C. I, IV, V, II, III   D. V, III, I, IV, II

   2.____

3.
   I. Many relish the opportunity to buy presents because gift-giving offers a powerful means to build stronger bonds with one's closest peers.
   II. Aside from purchasing holiday gifts, most people regularly buy presents for other occasions throughout the year, including weddings, birthdays, anniversaries, graduations, and baby showers.
   III. Last year, Americans spent over $30 billion at retail stores in the month of December alone.
   IV. This frequent experience of gift-giving can engender ambivalent feelings in gift-givers.
   V. Every day, millions of shoppers hit the stores in full force—both online and on foot—searching frantically for the perfect gift.
   The CORRECT answer is:
   A. II, III, V, I, IV   B. IV, V, I, III, II   C. III, II, V, I, IV   D. V, III, II, IV, I

   3.____

4. I. Why do gift-givers assume that gift price is closely linked to gift-recipients' feelings of appreciation?
    II. Perhaps givers believe that bigger (i.e., more expensive) gifts convey stronger signals of thoughtfulness and consideration.
    III. In this sense, gift-givers may be motivated to spend more money on a gift in order to send a "stronger signal" to their intended recipient.
    IV. According to Camerer (1988) and others, gift-giving represents a symbolic ritual, whereby gift-givers attempt to signal their positive attitudes toward the intended recipient and their willingness to invest resources in a future relationship.
    V. As for gift-recipients, they may not construe smaller and larger gifts as representing smaller and larger signals of thoughtfulness and consideration.
    The CORRECT answer is:
    A. V, III, II, IV, I   B. I, II, IV, III, V   C. IV, I, III, V, II   D. II, V, I, IV, III

5. I. But when the spider is not hungry, the stimulation of its hairs merely causes it to shake the touched limb.
    II. Touching this body hair produces one of two distinct reactions.
    III. The entire body of a tarantula, especially its legs, is thickly clothed with hair.
    IV. Some of it is short and wooly, some long and stiff.
    V. When the spider is hungry, it responds with an immediate and swift attack.
    The CORRECT answer is:
    A. IV, II, I, III, V   B. V, I, III, IV, II   C. III, IV, II, V, I   D. I, II, IV, III, V

6. I. That tough question may be just one question away from an easy one.
    II. They tend to be arranged sequentially: questions on the first paragraph come before questions on the second paragraph.
    III. In summation, it is important not to forget that there is no penalty for guessing.
    IV. Try *all* questions on the passage.
    V. Remember, the critical reading questions after each passage are not arranged in order of difficulty.
    The CORRECT answer is:
    A. I, III, IV, II, V   B. II, I, V, III, IV   C. III, IV, I, V, II   D. V, II, IV, I, III

7. I. This time of year clients come to me with one goal in mind: losing weight.
    II. I usually tell them that their goal should be focused on fat loss instead of weight loss.
    III. Converting and burning fat while maintaining or building muscle is an art, which also happens to be my job.
    IV. What I love about this line of work is that *everyone* benefits from healthy eating and supplemental nutrition.
    V. This is because most of us have more stored fat than we prefer, but we do not want to lose muscle in addition to the fat.
    The CORRECT answer is:
    A. V, III, I, II, IV   B. I, IV, V, III, IV   C. II, I, III, IV, V   D. II, V, IV, I, II

3 (#1)

8.
I. In Tierra del Fuego, "invasive" describes the beaver perfectly.
II. What started as a small influx of 50 beavers has since grown to a number over 200,000.
III. Unlike in North America where the beaver has several natural predators that help to maintain manageable population numbers, Tierra del Fuego has no such luxury.
IV. An invasive species is a non-indigenous animal, fungus, or plant species introduced to an area that has the potential to inflict harm upon the native ecosystem.
V. It was first introduced in 1946 by the Argentine government in an effort to catalyze a fur trading industry in the region.
The CORRECT answer is:
A. IV, I, V, II, III   B. I, IV, II, III, V   C. II, V, III, I, IV   D. V, II, IV, III, I

8.____

9.
I. The words ensure that we are all part of something much larger than the here and now.
II. Literature might be thought of as the creative measure of history.
III. It seems impossible to disconnect most literary works from their historical context.
IV. Great writers, poets, and playwrights mold their sense of life and the events of their time into works of art.
V. However, the themes that make their work universal and enduring perhaps do transcend time.
The CORRECT answer is:
A. I, III, II, V, IV   B. IV, I, V, II, III   C. II, IV, III, V, I   D. III, V, I, IV, II

9.____

10.
I. If you don't already have an exercise routine, try to build up to a good 20- to 45-minute aerobic workout.
II. When your brain is well oxygenated, it works more efficiently, so you do your work better and faster.
III. Your routine will help you enormously when you sit down to work on homework or even on the day of a test.
IV. Twenty minutes of cardiovascular exercise is a great warm-up before you start your homework.
V. Exercise does not just help your muscles; it also helps your brain.
The CORRECT answer is:
A. I, IV, II, IV, III   B. IV, V, II, I, III   C. V, III, IV, II, I   D. III, IV, I, V, II

10.____

11.
I. Experts often suggest that crime resembles an epidemic, but what kind?
II. If it travels along major transportation routes, the cause is microbial.
III. Economics professor Karl Smith has a good rule of thumb for categorizing epidemics: if it is along the lines of communication, he says the cause is information.
IV. However, if it spreads everywhere all at once, the cause is a molecule.
V. If it spreads out like a fan, the cause is an insect.
The CORRECT answer is:
A. I, III, II, V, IV   B. II, I, V, IV, III   C. V, III, I, II, IV   D. IV, V, I, III, II

11.____

12. I. A recent study had also suggested a link between childhood lead exposure and juvenile delinquency later on.
    II. These ideas all caused Nevin to look into other sources of lead-based items as well, such as gasoline.
    III. In 1994, Rick Nevin was a consultant working for the U.S Department of Housing and Urban Development on the costs and benefits of removing lead paint from old houses.
    IV. Maybe reducing lead exposure could have an effect on violent crime too?
    V. A growing body of research had linked lead exposure in small children with a whole raft of complications later in life, including lower IQ and behavioral problems.
    The CORRECT answer is:
    A. I, III, V, II, IV   B. IV, I, II, V, III   C. I, III, V, IV, II   D. III, V, I, IV, II

12.____

13. I. Like Lord Byron a century earlier, he had learn to play himself, his own best hero, with superb conviction.
    II. Or maybe he was Tarzan Hemingway, crouching in the African bush with elephant gun at the ready.
    III. He was Hemingway of the rugged outdoor grin and the hairy chest posing beside the lion he had just shot.
    IV. But even without the legend, the chest-beating, wisecracking pose that was later to seem so absurd, his impact upon us was tremendous.
    V. By the time we were old enough to read Hemingway, he had become legendary.
    The CORRECT answer is:
    A. I, V, II, IV, III   B. II, I, III, IV, V   C. IV, II, V, III, I   D. V, I, III, II, IV

13.____

14. I. Why do the electrons that inhabit atoms jump around so strangely, from one bizarrely shaped orbital to another?
    II. And most importantly, why do protons, the bits that give atoms their heft and personality, stick together at all?
    III. Why are some atoms, like sodium, so hyperactive while others, like helium, are so aloof?
    IV. As any good contractor will tell you, a sound structure requires stable materials.
    V. But atoms, the building blocks of everything we know and love—brownies and butterflies and beyond—do not appear to be models of stability.
    The CORRECT answer is:
    A. IV, V, III, I, II   B. V, III, I, II, IV   C. I, IV, II, V, III   D. III, I, IV, II, V

14.____

15. I. Current atomic theory suggests that the strong nuclear force is most likely conveyed by massless particles called "gluons".
    II. According to quantum chromodynamics (QCD), protons and neutrons are composed of smaller particles called quarks, which are held together by the gluons.
    III. As a quantum theory, it conceives of space and time as tiny chunks that occasionally misbehave, rather than smooth predictable quantities.

15.____

IV. If you are hoping that QCD ties up atomic behavior with a tidy little bow, you will be disappointed.

V. This quark-binding force has "residue" that extends beyond protons and neutrons themselves to provide enough force to bind the protons and neutrons together.

The CORRECT answer is:
A. III, IV, II, V, I   B. II, I, IV, III, V   C. I, II, V, IV, III   D. V, III, I, IV, II

16.
I. I have seen him whip a woman, causing the blood to run half an hour at a time.
II. Mr. Severe, the overseer, used to stand by the door of the quarter, armed with a large hickory stick, ready to whip anyone who was not ready to start at the sound of the horn.
III. This was in the midst of her crying children, pleading for their mother's release.
IV. He seemed to take pleasure in manifesting his fiendish barbarity.
V. Mr. Severe was rightly named: he was a cruel man.

The CORRECT answer is:
A. I, IV, III, II, I   B. II, V, I, III, IV   C. II, V, III, I, IV   D. IV, III, I, V, II

17.
I. His death was recorded by the slaves as the result of a merciful providence.
II. His career was cut short.
III. He died very soon after I went to Colonel Lloyd's; and he died as he lived, uttering bitter curses and horrid oaths.
IV. Mr. Severe's place was filled by a Mr. Hopkins.
V. From the rising till the going down of the sun, he was cursing, raving, cutting, and slashing among the slaves in the field.

The CORRECT answer is:
A. V, II, III, I, IV   B. IV, I, III, II, V   C. III, I, IV, V, II   D. I, II, V, III, IV

18.
I. The primary reef-building organisms are invertebrate animals known as corals.
II. They are located in warm, shallow, tropical marine waters with enough light to stimulate the growth of reef organisms.
III. Coral reefs are highly diverse ecosystems, supporting greater numbers of fish species than any other marine ecosystem.
IV. They belong to the class Anthozoa and are subdivided into stony corals, which have six tentacles.
V. These corals are small colonial, marine invertebrates.

The CORRECT answer is:
A. I, IV, V, II, III   B. V, I, III, IV, II   C. III, II, I, V, IV   D. IV, V, II, III, I

19.
I. Jane Goodall, an English ethologist, is famous for her studies of the chimpanzees of the Gombe Stream Reserve in Tanzania.
II. As a result of her studies, Goodall concluded that chimpanzees are an advanced species closely related to humans.
III. Ultimately, Goodall's observations led her to write *The Chimpanzee Family Book*, which conveys a new, more humane view of wildlife.

IV. She is credited with the first recorded observation of chimps eating meat and using and making tools.
V. Her observations have forced scientists to redefine the characteristics once considered as solely human traits.
The CORRECT answer is:
A. V, II, IV, III, I   B. I, IV, II, V, III   C. I, II, V, IV, III   D. III, V, II, I, IV

20. I. Since then, research has demonstrated that the deposition of atmospheric chemicals is causing widespread acidification of lakes, streams, and soil.
II. "Acid rain" is a popularly used phrase that refers to the deposition of acidifying substances from the atmosphere.
III. This phenomenon became a prominent issue around 1970.
IV. Of the many chemicals that are deposited from the atmosphere, the most important in terms of causing acidity in soil and surface waters are dilute solutions of sulfuric and nitric acids.
V. These chemicals are deposited as acidic rain or snow and include sulfur dioxide, oxides of nitrogen, and tiny particulates such as ammonium sulfate.
The CORRECT answer is:
A. III, IV, I, II, V   B. IV, III, I, IV, V   C. V, I, IV, III, II   D. II, III, I, IV, V

21. I. Programmers wrote algorithmic software that precisely specified both the problem and how to solve it.
II. AI programmers, in contrast, have sought to program computers with flexible rules for seeking solutions to problems.
III. In the 1940 and 1950s, the first large, electronic, digital computers were designed to perform numerical calculations set up by a human programmer.
IV. The computers did so by completing a series of clearly defined steps, or algorithms.
V. An AI program may be designed to modify the rules it is given or to develop entirely new rules.
The CORRECT answer is:
A. I, III, II, V, IV   B. IV, I, III, V, II   C. III, IV, I, II, V   D. III, I, II, IV, V

22. I. Wildfire is a periodic ecological disturbance, associated with the rapid combustion of much of the biomass of an ecosystem.
II. Wildfires themselves are both routine and ecologically necessary.
III. It is where they encounter human habitation, of course, that dangers quickly escalate,
IV. Once ignited by lightning or by humans, the biomass oxidizes as an uncontrolled blaze.
V. This unfettered burning continues until the fire either runs out of fuel or is quenched.
The CORRECT answer is:
A. V, IV, I, II, III   B. I, II, V, III, IV   C. III, II, I, IV, V   D. IV, V, III, I, II

23. I. His arguments supported the positions advanced by the Democratic Party's southern wing and sharply challenged the constitutionality of the Republican Party's emerging political platform.
     II. Beginning in the mid-1840s as a simple freedom suit, the case ended with the Court's intervention in the central political issues of the 1850s and the intensification of the sectional crisis that ultimately led to civil war.
     III. During the Civil War, the decision quickly fell into disrepute, and its major rulings were overruled by ratification of the 13th and 14th Amendments.
     IV. *Dred Scott v. Sandford* ranks as one of the worst decisions in the Supreme Court's history.
     V. Chief Justice Roger Taney, speaking for a deeply divided Court, brought about this turn of events by ruling that no black American—whether free or enslaved—could be a U.S. citizen and that Congress possessed no legitimate authority to prohibit slavery's expansion into the federal territories.
     The CORRECT answer is:
     A. II, IV, I, III, V   B. V, I, III, IV, II   C. I, V, II, V, III   D. IV, II, V, I, III

24. I. Considered the last battle between the U.S. Army and American Indians, the Wounded Knee Massacre took place on the morning of 29 December 1890 beside Wounded Knee Creek on South Dakota's Pine Ridge Reservation.
     II. This was the culmination of the Ghost Dance religion that had started with a Paiute prophet from Nevada named Wovoka (1856-1932), who was also known as Jack Wilson.
     III. During the previous year, U.S. government officials had reduced Sioux lands and cut back rations so severely that the Sioux people were starving.
     IV. These conditions encouraged the desperate embrace of the Ghost Dance.
     V. This pan-tribal ritual had historical antecedents that go much further back than its actual founder.
     The CORRECT answer is:
     A. I, II, III, IV, V   B. V, IV, II, III, I   C. IV, III, I, V, II   D. III, I, V, II, IV

25. I. Their actions, which became known as the Boston Tea Party, set in motion events that led directly to the American Revolution.
     II. Urged on by a crowd of cheering townspeople, the disguised Bostonians destroyed 342 chests of tea estimated to be worth between $10,000 an $18,000.
     III. The Americans, who numbered around 70, shared a common aim: to destroy the ships' cargo of British East India Company tea.
     IV. Many years later, George Hewes, a 31-year-old shoemaker and participant, recalled "We then were ordered by our commander to open the hatches and take out all the chests of tea and throw them overboard. And we immediately proceeded to execute his orders, first cutting and splitting the chests with our tomahawks, so as thoroughly to expose them to the effects of the water.

V. At nine o'clock on the night of December 16, 1773, a band of Bostonians disguised as Native Americans boarded the British merchant ship Dartmouth and two companion vessels anchored at Griffin's Wharf in Boston harbor.

The CORRECT answer is:

A. V, III, IV, II, I B. IV, II, III, I, V C. III, IV, V, II, I D. V, II, IV, III, I

KEY (CORRECT ANSWERS)

1. A
2. C
3. D
4. B
5. C

6. D
7. B
8. A
9. C
10. B

11. A
12. D
13. D
14. A
15. C

16. B
17. A
18. C
19. B
20. D

21. C
22. B
23. D
24. A
25. A

TEST 2

DIRECTIONS: The sentences listed below are part of a meaningful paragraph, but they are not given in their proper order. You are to decide what would be the BEST order to put sentences to form a well-organized paragraph. Each sentence has a place in the paragraph; there are no extra sentences. *PRINT THE LETTER OF THE CORRECT ANSWER IN THE SPACE AT THE RIGHT.*

1.
   I. Recently, some U.S. cities have added a new category: compost, organic matter such as food scraps and yard debris.
   II. For example, paper may go in one container, glass and aluminum in another, regular garbage in a third.
   III. Like paper or glass recycling, compositing demands a certain amount of effort from the public in order to be successful.
   IV. Over the past generation, people in many parts of the United States have become accustomed to dividing their household waste products into different categories for recycling.
   V. But the inconveniences of composting are far outweighed by its benefits.
   The CORRECT answer is:
   A. V, II, III, IV, I   B. I, III, IV, V, II   C. IV, II, I, III, V   D. III, I, V, II, IV

1.____

2.
   I. It also enhances soil texture, encouraging healthy roots and minimizing the need for chemical fertilizers.
   II. Most people think of banana peels, eggshells, and dead leaves as "waste," but compost is actually a valuable resource with multiple practical uses.
   III. When utilized as a garden fertilizer, compost provides nutrients to soil and improves plant growth while deterring or killing pests and preventing some plant diseases.
   IV. In large quantities, compost can be converted into a natural gas that can be used as fuel for transportation or heating and cooling systems.
   V. Better than soil at holding moisture, compost minimizes water waste and storm runoff, increases savings on watering costs, and helps reduce erosion on embankments near bodies of water.
   The CORRECT answer is:
   A. II, III, I, V, IV   B. I, IV, V, III, II   C. V, II, IV, I, III   D. III, V, II, IV, I

2.____

3.
   I. The street is a sea of red, the traditional Chinese color of luck and happiness.
   II. Buildings are draped with festive, red banners and garlands.
   III. Crowds gather then to celebrate Lunar New Year.
   IV. Lamp posts are strung with crimson paper lanterns, which bob in the crisp winter breeze.
   V. At the beginning of February, thousands of people line H Street, the heart of Chinatown in Washington, D.C.
   The CORRECT answer is:
   A. I, V, II, III, IV   B. IV, II, V, I, III   C. III, I, II, IV, V   D. V, III, I, II, IV

3.____

4. I. Experts agree that the lion dance originated in the Han dynasty; however, there is little agreement about the dance's original purpose.
   II. Another theory is that an emperor, upon waking from a dream about a lion, hired an artist to choreograph the dance.
   III. Dancers must be synchronized with the music accompanying the dance, as well as with each other, in order to fully realize the celebration.
   IV. Whatever the origins are, the current function of the dance is celebration.
   V. Some evidence suggests that the earliest version of the dance was an attempt to ward off an evil spirt.
   The CORRECT answer is:
   A. V, II, IV, III, I   B. I, V, II, IV, III   C. II, I, III, V, IV   D. IV, III, V, I, II

4.____

5. I. Half the population of New York, Toronto, and London do not own cars; instead they use public transport.
   II. Every day, subway systems carry 155 million passengers, thirty-four times the number carried by all the world's airplanes.
   III. Though there are 600 million cars on the planet, and counting, there are also seven billion people, which means most of us get around taking other modes of transportation.
   IV. All of that is to say that even a century and a half after the invention of the internal combustion engine, private car ownership is still an anomaly.
   V. In other words, traveling to work, school, or the market means being a straphanger: someone who relies on public transport.
   The CORRECT answer is:
   A. I, II, IV, V, III   B. III, V, I, II, IV   C. III, I, II, IV, V   D. II, IV, V, III, I

5.____

6. I. "They jumped up like popcorn," he said, describing how they would flap their half-formed wings and take short hops into the air.
   II. Dan settled on the Chukar Partridge as a model species, but he might not have made his discovery without the help of a local rancher that supplied him with the birds.
   III. At field sites around the world, Dan Kiel saw a pattern in how young ground birds ran along behind their parents.
   IV. So when a group of graduate students challenged him to come up with new data on the age-old ground-up-tree-down debate, he designed a project to see what clues might lie in how baby game birds learned to fly.
   V. When the rancher stopped by to see how things were progressing, he yelled at Dan to give the birds something to climb on.
   The CORRECT answer is:
   A. IV, II, V, I, III   B. III, II, I, V, IV   C. III, I, IV, II, V   D. I, II, IV, V, III

6.____

7. I. Honey bees are hosts to the pathogenic large ectoparasitic mite, *Varroa destructor*.
   II. These mites feed on bee hemolymph (blood) and can kill bees directly or by increasing their susceptibility to secondary infections.
   III. Little is known about the natural defenses that keep the mite infections under control.

7.____

IV. Pyrethrums are a group of flowering plants that produce potent insecticides with anti-mite activity.
V. In fact, the human mite infestation known as scabies is treated with a topical pyrethrum cream.
The CORRECT answer is:
A. I, II, III, IV, V   B. V, IV, II, I, III   C. III, IV, V, I, II   D. II, IV, I, III, V

8. I. He hardly ever allowed me to pay for the books he placed in my hands, but when he wasn't looking I'd leave the coins I'd managed to collect on the counter.
    II. My favorite place in the whole city was the Sempere & Sons bookshop on Calle Santa Ana.
    III. It smelled of old paper and dust and it was my sanctuary, my refuge.
    IV. The bookseller would let me sit on a chair in a corner and read any book I liked to my heart's content.
    V. It was only small change—if I'd had to buy a book with that pittance, I would probably have been able to afford only a booklet of cigarette papers.
    The CORRECT answer is:
    A. I, III, V, II, IV   B. II, IV, I, III, V   C. V, I, III, IV, II   D. II, III, IV, I, V

9. I. At school, I had learned to read and write long before the other children.
    II. My father, however, did not see things the way I did; he did not like to see books in the house.
    III. Where my school friends saw notches of ink on incomprehensible pages, I saw light, streets, and people.
    IV. Back then my only friends were made of paper and ink.
    V. Words and the mystery of their hidden science fascinated me, and I saw in them a key with which I could unlock a boundless world.
    The CORRECT answer is:
    A. IV, I, III, V, II   B. I, V, III, IV, II   C. II, I, V, III, IV   D. V, IV, II, III, I

10. I. Gary King of Harvard University says that one main reason null results are not published is because there were many ways to produce them by messing up.
    II. Oddly enough, there is little hard data on how often or why null results are squelched.
    III. The various errors make the null reports almost impossible to predict, Mr. King believes.
    IV. In recent years, the debate has spread to social and behavioral science, which help sway public and social policy.
    V. The question of what to do with null results in research has long been hotly debated among those conducting medical trials.
    The CORRECT answer is:
    A. I, III, IV, V, II   B. V, I, II, IV, III   C. III, II, I, V, IV   D. V, IV, II, I, III

11.
   I. In a recent study, Stanford political economist Neil Malholtra and two of his graduate students examined all studies funded by TESS (Time-sharing Experiments for Social Sciences).
   II. Scientists of these experiments cited deeper problems within their studies but also believed many journalists wouldn't be interested in their findings.
   III. TESS allows scientists to order up internet-based surveys of a representative sample of U.S. adults to test a particular hypothesis.
   IV. One scientist went on record as saying, "The reality is that null effects do not tell a clear story."
   V. Well, Malholtra's team tracked down working papers from most of the experiments that weren't published to find out what had happened to their results.

   The CORRECT answer is:
   A. IV, II, V, III, I   B. I, III, V, II, IV   C. III, V, I, IV, II   D. I, III, IV, II, V

12.
   I. The work also suggests that these ultra-tiny salt wires may already exist in sea spray and large underground salt deposits.
   II. Scientists expect for metals such as gold or lead to stretch out at temperatures well below their melting points, but they never expected this superplasticity in a rigid, crystalline material like salt.
   III. Inflexible old salt becomes a softy in the nanoworld, stretching like taffy to more than twice its length, researchers report.
   IV. The findings may lead to new approaches for making nanowires that could end up in solar cells or electronic circuits.
   V. According to Nathan Moore of Sandia National Laboratories, these nanowires are special and much more common than we may think.

   The CORRECT answer is:
   A. IV, III, V, II, I   B. I, V, III, IV, II   C. III, IV, I, V, II   D. V, II, III, I, IV

13.
   I. The Venus flytrap (Dionaea muscipula) needs to know when an ideal meal is crawling across its leaves.
   II. The large black hairs on their lobes allow the Venus flytraps to literally feel their prey, and they act as triggers that spring the trap closed.
   III. To be clear, if an insect touches just one hair, the trap will not spring shut; but a large enough bug will likely touch two hairs within twenty seconds which is the signal the Venus flytrap waits for.
   IV. Closing its trap requires a huge expense of energy, and reopening can take several hours.
   V. When the proper prey makes its way across the trap, the Dionaea launches into action.

   The CORRECT answer is:
   A. IV, I, V, II, III   B. II, V, I, III, IV   C. I, II, V, IV, III   D. I, IV, II, V, III

14. I. These books usually contain collections of stories, many of which are much older than the books themselves.
     II. Where other early European authors wrote their literary works in Latin, the Irish began writing down their stories in their own language as early as 6th century B.C.E.
     III. Ireland has the oldest vernacular literature in Europe.
     IV. One of the most famous of these collections is the epic cycle, *The Táin Bó Culainge*, which translates to "The Cattle Raid of Cooley."
     V. While much of the earliest Irish writing has been lost or destroyed, several manuscripts survive from the late medieval period.
     The CORRECT answer is:
     A. V, IV, I, II, III   B. III, II, V, I, IV   C. III, I, IV, V, II   D. IV, II, III, I, V

15. I. Obviously the plot is thin, but it works better as a thematic peace, exploring several great issues that plagued authors and people during that era.
     II. The story begins during a raid when Meb's forces are joined by Frederick and his men.
     III. In the end, many warriors on both sides perish, the prize is lost, and peace is somehow re-established between the opposing sides.
     IV. The middle of the story tells of how Chulu fends off Meb's army by herself while Concho's men struggle against witchcraft.
     V. The prize is defended by the current king, Concho, and the young warrior, Chulu.
     The CORRECT answer is:
     A. II, V, IV, III, I   B. V, I, IV, III, II   C. I, III, V, IV, II   D. III, II, I, V, IV

16. I. However, sometimes the flowers that are treated with the pesticides are not as vibrant as those that did not receive the treatment.
     II. The first phase featured no pesticides and the second featured a pesticide that varied in doses.
     III. In the cultivation of roses, certain pesticides are often applied when the presence of aphids is detected.
     IV. Recently, researchers conducted two phases of an experiment to study the effects of certain pesticides on rose bushes.
     V. To start, aphids are small plant-eating insects known to feed on rose bushes.
     The CORRECT answer is:
     A. IV, III, II, I, V   B. I, II, V, III, IV   C. V, III, I, IV, II   D. II, V, IV, I, III

17. I. My passion for it took hold many years ago when I happened to cross paths with a hiker in a national park.
     II. The wilderness has a way of cleansing the spirit.
     III. His excitement was infectious as he quoted various poetic verses pertaining to the wild; I was hooked.
     IV. For some, backpacking is the ultimate vacation.
     V. While it once felt tedious and tiring, backpacking is now an essential part of my summer recreation.
     The CORRECT answer is:
     A. IV, II, V, I, III   B. II, III, I, IV, V   C. I, IV, II, V, III   D. V, I, III, II, IV

18. I. When I was preparing for my two-week vacation to southern Africa, I realized that the continent would be like nothing I have ever seen.
    II. I wanted to explore the continent's urban streets as well as the savannah; it's always been my dream to have "off the grid" experiences as well as touristy ones.
    III. The largest gap in understanding came from an unlikely source; it was the way I played with my host family's dog.
    IV. Upon my arrival to Africa, the people I met welcomed me with open arms.
    V. Aside from the pleasant welcome, it was obvious that our cultural differences were stark, which led to plenty of laughter and confusion.
    The CORRECT answer is:
    A. IV, I, II, III, V   B. III, V, IV, II, I   C. I, IV, II, III, V   D. I, II, IV, V, III

19. I. There, I signed up for a full-contact, downhill ice-skating race that looked like a bobsled run.
    II. It wasn't until I took a trip to Montreal that I realized how wrong I was.
    III. As an avid skier and inline skater, I figured I had cornered the market on downhill speeds.
    IV. After avoiding hip and body checks, both of which were perfectly legal, I was able to reach a top speed of forty-five miles per hour!
    V. It was Carnaval season, the time when people from across the province flock to the city for two weeks of food, drink and winter sports.
    The CORRECT answer is:
    A. II, I, III, IV, V   B. III, II, V, I, IV   C. IV, V, I, III, II   D. I, IV, II, V, III

20. I. It is a spell that sets upon one's soul and a sense of euphoria is felt by all who experience it.
    II. Pictures and postcards of the Caribbean do not lie; the water there shines with every shade of aquamarine, from pastel to emerald.
    III. As I imagine these sights, I recall one trip in particular that neatly captures the allure of the Caribbean.
    IV. The ocean hypnotizes with its glassy vastness.
    V. On that beautiful day, I was incredibly happy to sail with my family and friends.
    The CORRECT answer is:
    A. I, V, IV, III, II   B. V, I, II, IV, III   C. II, IV, I, III, V   D. I, II, IV, III, V

21. I. It wasn't until the early 1700s that it began to resemble the masterpiece museum it is today.
    II. The Louvre contains some of the most famous works of art in the history of the world including the *Mona Lisa* and the *Venus de Milo*.
    III. Before it was a world famous museum, The Louvre was a fort built by King Philip sometime around 1200 A.D.
    IV. The Louvre, in Paris, France, is one of the largest museums in the world.
    V. It has almost 275,000 works of art, which are displayed in over 140 exhibition rooms.
    The CORRECT answer is:
    A. V, I, III, IV, II   B. II, IV, I, V, III   C. V, III, I, IV, II   D. IV, V, II, III, I

22. I. It danced on the glossy hair and bright eyes of two girls, who sat together hemming ruffles for a white muslin dress.
    II. The September sun was glinting cheerfully into a pretty bedroom furnished with blue.
    III. These girls were Clover and Elsie Carr, and it was Clover's first evening dress for which they were hemming ruffles.
    IV. The half-finished skirt of the dress lay on the bed, and as each crisp ruffle was completed, the girls added it to the snowy heap, which looked like a drift of transparent clouds.
    V. It was nearly two years since a certain visit made by Johnnie to Inches Mills and more than three since Clover and Katy had returned home from the boarding school at Hillsover.
    The CORRECT answer is:
    A. III, V, IV, I, II   B. II, I, IV, III, V   C. V, II, I, IV, III   D. II, IV, III, I, V

23. I. The "invisible hand" theory is harshly criticized by parties who argue that untampered self-interest is immoral and that charity is the superior vehicle for community improvement.
    II. Standing as a testament to his benevolence, Smith bequeathed much of his wealth to charity.
    III. Second, Smith was not arguing that all self-interest is positive for society; he simply did not agree that it was necessarily bad.
    IV. First, he was not declaring that people should adopt a pattern of overt self-interest, but rather that people already act in such a way.
    V. Some of these people, though, fail to recognize several important aspects of Adam Smith's the Scottish economist who championed this theory, concept.
    The CORRECT answer is:
    A. I, V, IV, III, II   B. III, IV, II, I, V   C. II, III, V, IV, I   D. IV, III, I, V, II

24. I. Though they rarely are awarded for their many accomplishments, composers and performers continue to innovate and represent a substantial reason for classical music's persistent popularity.
    II. It is often the subject of experimentation on the part of composers and performers.
    III. Even more restrictive is the mainstream definition of "classical," which only includes the music of generations past that has seemingly been pushed aside by such contemporary forms of music as jazz, rock, and rap.
    IV. In spite of its waning limelight, however, classical music occupies an enduring niche in Western culture.
    V. Many people take classical music to be the realm of the symphony orchestra or smaller ensembles of orchestral instruments.
    The CORRECT answer is:
    A. IV, I, III, II, V   B. II, IV, V, I, III   C. V, III, IV, II, I   D. I, V, III, IV, II

25. I. The Great Pyramid at Giza is arguably one of the most fascinating and contentious pieces of architecture in the world.
    II. Instead of clarifying or expunging older theories about its age, the results of the study left the researchers mystified.
    III. In the 1980s, researchers began focusing on studying the mortar from the pyramid, hoping it would reveal important clues about the pyramid's age and construction.
    IV. This discovery was controversial because these dates claimed that the structure was built over 400 years earlier than most archaeologists originally believed it had been constructed.
    V. Carbon dating revealed that the pyramid had been built between 3100 BCE and 2850 BCE with an average date of 2977 BCE.
    The CORRECT answer is:
    A. I, III, II, V, IV   B. II, III, IV, V, I   C. V, I, III, IV, II   D. III, IV, V, I, II

25.____

KEY (CORRECT ANSWERS)

1. C
2. A
3. D
4. B
5. B

6. C
7. A
8. D
9. A
10. D

11. B
12. C
13. D
14. B
15. A

16. C
17. A
18. D
19. B
20. C

21. D
22. B
23. A
24. C
25. A

EXAMINATION SECTION

TEST 1

DIRECTIONS: The sentences listed below are part of a meaningful paragraph, but they are not given in their proper order. You are to decide what would be the BEST order to put sentences to form a well-organized paragraph. Each sentence has a place in the paragraph; there are no extra sentences. *PRINT THE LETTER OF THE CORRECT ANSWER IN THE SPACE AT THE RIGHT.*

Questions 1-3.

DIRECTIONS: Questions 1 through 3 are to be answered on the basis of the following passage.

Almost half of the increase in Chicago came from five neighborhoods, including West Garfield Park. He was 12 years old and had just been recruited into a gang by his older brothers and cousin. A decade later, he sits in Cook County jail, held without bail and awaiting trial on three cases, including felony drug charges and possession of a weapon. Violence in Chicago erupted last year, with the city recording 771 murders—a 58% jump from 2015. They point to a $95 million police-training center in West Garfield Park, public-transit improvements on Chicago's south side and efforts to get major corporations such as Whole Foods and Wal-Mart to invest. Chicago city officials say that they are making strategic investments in ailing neighborhoods. Amarley Coggins remembers the first time he dealt heroin, discreetly approaching a car coming off an interstate highway and into West Garfield park, the neighborhood where he grew up on Chicago's west side.

1. When organized correctly, the first sentence of the paragraph begins with 1.____
   A. "Amarley Coggins remembers..."   B. "He was 12 years old..."
   C. "They point to a..."   D. "Violence in Chicago..."

2. After correctly organizing the paragraph, the author wishes to replace a word 2.____
   in the last sentence with its synonym *enterprises*. Which word does the author wish to replace?
   A. murders   B. neighborhoods
   C. corporations   D. improvements

3. If put together correctly, the second to last sentence would end with the words 3.____
   A. "...Chicago's west side."   B. "...in ailing neighborhoods."
   C. "...older brother and cousins."   D. "...and Wal-Mart to invest."

Questions 4-6.

DIRECTIONS: Questions 4 through 6 are to be answered on the basis of the following passage.

Critics argue that driverless vehicles pose too many risks, including cyberattacks, computer malfunctions, relying on algorithms to make ethical decisions, and fewer transportation jobs. Driverless vehicles, also called autonomous vehicles and self-driving vehicles, are vehicles that can operate without human intervention. And algorithms make decisions based on data obtained from sensors and connectivity. Driverless vehicles rely primarily on three technologies: sensors, connectivity, and algorithms. Sensors observe multiple directions simultaneously. Connectivity accesses information on traffic, weather, road hazards, and navigation. Supporters argue that driverless vehicles have many benefits, including fewer traffic accidents and fatalities, more efficient traffic flows, greater mobility for those who cannot drive, and less pollution. Once the realm of science fiction, driverless vehicles could revolutionize automotive travel over the next few decades.

4. When all of the sentences are organized in correct order, the first sentence starts with
    A. "Connectivity accesses information…"
    B. "Critics argue that…"
    C. "Once the realm of…"
    D. "Driverless vehicles, also called…"

4._____

5. If the above paragraph appeared in correct order, which of the following transition words would be MOST appropriate in the beginning of the sentence that starts "Critics argue that…"
    A. Additionally
    B. To begin,
    C. In conclusion,
    D. Conversely,

5._____

6. When the paragraph is properly arranged, it ends with the words
    A. "…over the next few decades."
    B. "…fewer transportation jobs."
    C. "…and less pollution."
    D. "…without human intervention"

6._____

Questions 7-10.

DIRECTIONS: Questions 7 through 10 are to be answered on the basis of the following passage.

This method had some success, but also carried fatal risks. Various people across Europe independently developed vaccination as an alternative during the later years of the eighteenth century, but Edward Jenner (1749-1823) popularized the practice. Vaccination has been called a miracle of modern medicine, but it has a long and controversial history stretching back to the ancient world. In 1803 the Royal Jennerian Institute was founded in England, and vaccination programs initially drew enormous public support. In 429 BCE in Greece, the historian Thucydides (c.460-c.395 BCE) noted that survivors of smallpox did not become reinfected in subsequent epidemics. Variolation as a means of preventing severe smallpox infection became an accepted practice in China in the tenth century CE, and its popularity spread across Asia,

Europe, and to the Americas by the seventeenth century. Variolation required either inhalation of smallpox dust, or putting scabs or parts of the smallpox pustules under the skin. Widespread inoculation against smallpox was purported to have been part of Ayurvedic tradition as far back as at least 1000 BCE, when Indian doctors traveled to households before the rainy season each year.

7. When arranged properly, what does "This method" refer to in the sentence that begins "This method had some success..."? 7.____
    A. Vaccination
    B. Inoculation
    C. Variolation
    D. Hybridization

8. When organized correctly, the paragraph's third sentence should begin 8.____
    A. "In 429 BCE in Greece..."
    B. "Variolation required..."
    C. "In 1803 the..."
    D. "Vaccination has been called..."

9. If put in the correct order, this paragraph should end with the words 9.____
    A. "...under the skin."
    B. "...to the ancient world."
    C. "...enormous public support."
    D. "...by the seventeenth century."

10. In the second sentence, the author is thinking about using the word immunization instead of which of its synonyms? 10.____
    A. Variolation   B. Vaccination   C. Inhalation   D. Inoculation

Questions 11-13.

DIRECTIONS: Questions 11 through 13 are to be answered on the basis of the following passage.

Summers are hot—often north of 100 degrees—and because it lies at the far end of a San Diego Gas & Electric transmission line, the town has suffered frequent power outages. Another way is that microgrids can ease the entry of intermittent renewable energy sources, like wind and solar, into the modern grid. Utilities are also interested in microgrids because of the money they can save by deferring the need to build new transmission lines. "If you're on the very end of a utility line, everything that happens, happens 10 times worse for you," says Mike Gravely, team leader for energy systems integration at the California Energy Commission. The town has a lot of senior citizens, who can be frail in the heat. Borrego Springs, California, is a quaint town of about 3,400 people set against the Anza-Borrego Desert about 90 miles east of San Diego. High winds, lightning strikes, forest fires and flash floods can bust up that line and kill the electricity. But today, Borrego Springs has a failsafe against power outages: a microgrid. Resiliency is one of the main reasons the market in microgrids is booming, with installed capacity in the United States projected to be more than double between 2017 and 2022, according to a new report on microgrids from GTM Research. "Without air conditioning," says Linda Haddock, head of the local Chamber of Commerce, "people will die."

11. When the sentences above are organized correctly, the paragraph should start with the sentence that begins 11.____
    A. "Borrego Springs, California..."
    B. "But today, Borrego Springs..."
    C. "Summers are hot..."
    D. "Utilities are also interested..."

12. If the author wanted to split this paragraph into two smaller paragraphs, the first sentence of the second paragraph would start with the words
    A. "High winds, lightning strikes, forest fires…"
    B. "But today, Borrego Springs…"
    C. "Resiliency is one of the main…"
    D. "If you're on the very end…"

13. Assuming the paragraph were organized correctly, the second to last sentence would end
    A. "…to build new transmission lines."
    B. "…be frail in the heat."
    C. "…into the modern grid."
    D. "…east of San Diego."

Questions 14-17.

DIRECTIONS: Questions 14 through 17 are to be answered on the basis of the following passage.

Exhaustive search is not typically a successful approach to problem solving because most interesting problems have search spaces that are simply too large to be dealt with in this manner, even by the fastest computers. Thus, in order to ignore a portion of a search space, some guiding knowledge or insight must exist so that the solution will not be overlooked. This partial understanding is reflected in the fact that a rigid algorithmic solution—a routine and predetermined number of computational steps—cannot be applied. A large part of the intelligence of chess players resides in the heuristics they employ. When search is used to explore the entire solution space, it is said to be exhaustive. Chess is a classic example where humans routinely employ sophisticated heuristics in a search space. Therefore, if one hopes to find a solution (or a reasonably good approximation of a solution) to such a problem, one must selectively explore the problem's search space. Rather, the concept of search is used to solve such problems. Heuristics is a major area of AI that concerns itself with how to limit effectively the exploration of a search space. Many problems that humans are confronted with are not fully understood. The difficulty here is that if part of the search space is not explored, one runs the risk that the solution one seeks will be missed. A chess player will typically search through a small number of possible moves before selecting a move to play. Not every possible move and countermove sequence is explored. Only reasonable sequences are examined.

14. When correctly organized, the paragraph above should begin with the words
    A. "Many problems that…"
    B. "Therefore, if one hopes to…"
    C. "Only reasonable sequences are…"
    D. "The difficulty here is…"

15. If the paragraph was organized correctly, the fourth sentence would begin with the words
    A. "Chess is a classic…"   B. "Heuristics is a major…"
    C. "Exhaustive search is not…" D. "The difficulty here is…"

16. If the author wished to separate this paragraph into two equally sized paragraphs, the sentence that begins the second paragraph would END with the words
    A. "…heuristics they employ."
    B. "…in a search space."
    C. "…are not fully employed."
    D. "…will be missed."

    16._____

17. When organized correctly, the paragraph would end with the words
    A. "…the heuristics they employ."
    B. "…will not be overlooked."
    C. "…said to be exhaustive."
    D. "…are not fully understood."

    17._____

Questions 18-21.

DIRECTIONS: Questions 18 through 21 are to be answered on the basis of the following passage.

Asian-Americans soon found themselves the targets of ridicule and attacks. Prior to the bombing he had tried to enlist in the military but was turned down due to poor health. His case, Korematsu v. The United States, is still considered a blemish on the record of the Supreme Court and has received heightened scrutiny given the indefinite confinement of many prisoners after the terrorist attacks on September 11, 2001. On February 19, 1942, President Franklin D. Roosevelt issued Executive Order 9066, which granted the leaders of the armed forces permission to create Military Areas and authorizing the removal of any and all persons from those areas. Fred Korematsu was a 22-year-old welder when the Japanese bombed Pearl Harbor on December 7, 1941. A Nisei—which means an American citizen born to Japanese parents—he was one of four brothers and grew up working in his parents' plant nursery in Oakland, California. This statement effectively pronounced Japanese-Americans on the West Coast as traitors because even though Executive Order 9066 allowed the military to remove any person from designated areas, only those of Japanese descent were ordered to leave. Before Pearl Harbor, he was employed by a defense contractor in California. At the time of the attack, he was having a picnic with his Italian-American girlfriend. Asian-American Fred Korematsu (1919-2005) is most remembered for challenging the legality of Japanese internment during World War II. It was for this simple reason that he eventually became known as a civil rights leader. American reaction to an attack on United States' soil was both swift and harsh. Awarded the Presidential Medal of Honor, he is considered a leader of the civil rights movement in the United States. Roosevelt justified these actions in the opening paragraph of the order by declaring, "the successful prosecution of the war requires every possible protection against espionage, and against sabotage to national-defense material, national-defenses premises and national-defense utilities." Years later he told the San Francisco Chronicle, "I was just living my life, and that's what I wanted to do."

18. When put together correctly, the above paragraph would begin with the words
    A. "It was for this simple reason…"
    B. "A Nisei—which means…"
    C. "Awarded the Presidential Medal of Honor…"
    D. "Asian-American Fred Korematsu…"

    18._____

19. If the author wished to separate this piece into two separate paragraphs, the sentence that would be the BEST way to start the second paragraph would begin with the words
    A. "Awarded the Presidential Medal of Honor…"
    B. "Fred Korematsu was a…"
    C. "Roosevelt justified these actions…"
    D. "Before Pearl Harbor, he was…"

19.____

20. In the sentence that begins "A Nisei—which means…", who does "he" refer to in the paragraph?
    A. Roosevelt
    B. A sibling of Korematsu
    C. Fred Korematsu
    D. Japanese-Americans on the West Coast

20.____

21. If organized correctly, the fourth sentence should begin with the words
    A. "At the time of the attack…"
    B. "His case, Korematsu v. The United States…"
    C. "Fred Korematsu was a…"
    D. "This statement effectively pronounced…"

21.____

22. When put together correctly, the last sentence of the paragraph should end with the words
    A. "…that's what I wanted to do."
    B. "…were ordered to leave."
    C. "…during World War II."
    D. "…was both swift and harsh."

22.____

Questions 23-25.

DIRECTIONS: Questions 23 through 25 are to be answered on the basis of the following passage.

Over the past two decades, her personal finances have been eroded by illness, divorce, the cost of raising two children, the housing bust, and the economic downturn. "There are more people attending college, more people taking out loans, and more people taking out a higher dollar amount of loans," says Matthew Ward, associate director of media relations at the New York Fed. Anderson, who is 57, told her complicated story at a recent Senate Aging Committee hearing (she's previously appeared on the CBS Evening News). Some 3 percent of U.S. households that are headed by a senior citizen now hold federal student debt, mostly debt they took on to finance their own educations, according to a new report from the Government Accountability Office (GAO), an independent agency. She hasn't been able to afford payments on her loans for nearly eight years. Rosemary Anderson has a master's degree, a good job at the University of California (Santa Cruz), and student loans that she could be paying off until she's 81. Student debt has risen across every age group over the past decade, according to a Federal Reserve Bank of New York analysis of credit report data… "As the baby boomers continue to move into retirement, the number of older Americans with defaulted loans will only continue to increase," the report warned. She first enrolled in college in her thirties.

23. When organized correctly, the first sentence should begin with the words
    A. "She first enrolled…"   B. "Anderson, who is 57…"
    C. "Some 3 percent of…"   D. "Rosemary Anderson has…"

24. If the author wished to split the paragraph into two paragraphs (not necessarily equal in length), the first sentence of the second paragraph would begin with the words
    A. "Some 3 percent of…"   B. "There are more people…"
    C. "Over the past two decades…"   D. "She first enrolled…"

25. When put in the correct order, the second to last sentence should end with the words
    A. "…an independent agency."   B. "…of credit report data."
    C. "…at the New York Fed."   D. "…in her thirties."

KEY (CORRECT ANSWERS)

1.	A		11.	A
2.	C		12.	B
3.	B		13.	C
4.	D		14.	A
5.	D		15.	C
6.	B		16.	D
7.	C		17.	A
8.	A		18.	D
9.	C		19.	B
10.	D		20.	C

21.	C
22.	B
23.	D
24.	A
25.	B

TEST 2

DIRECTIONS: The sentences listed below are part of a meaningful paragraph, but they are not given in their proper order. You are to decide what would be the BEST order to put sentences to form a well-organized paragraph. Each sentence has a place in the paragraph; there are no extra sentences. *PRINT THE LETTER OF THE CORRECT ANSWER IN THE SPACE AT THE RIGHT.*

Questions 1-3.

DIRECTIONS: Questions 1 through 3 are to be answered on the basis of the following passage.

According to the World Health Organization (WHO), exposure to ambient (outdoor) air pollution causes 3 million premature deaths around the world each year, largely due to heart and lung diseases. Air pollution also contributes to such environmental threats as smog, acid rain, depletion of the ozone layer, and global climate change. The U.S. Environmental Protection Agency (EPA) sets National Ambient Air Quality Standards (NAAQS) for those four pollutants as well as carbon monoxide (CO) and lead. The EPA also regulates 187 toxic air pollutants, such as asbestos, benzene, dioxin, and mercury. Finally, the EPA places limits on emissions of greenhouse gases like carbon dioxide (CO_2) and methane, which contribute to global climate change. The WHO has established Air Quality Guidelines (ACGs) to identify safe levels of exposure to the emission of four harmful air pollutants worldwide: particulate matter (PM), ozone (O_3), nitrogen dioxide (NO_2), and sulfur dioxide (SO_2). Since EPA criteria define the allowable concentrations of these six substances in ambient air throughout the United States, they are known as criteria air pollutants. Air pollution refers to the release into the air of chemicals and other substances, known as pollutants, that are potentially harmful to human health and the environment.

1. When organized correctly, the first sentence of this paragraph should begin   1.____
   A. "Air pollution refers…"
   B. "The EPA also regulates..,"
   C. "The WHO has established…"
   D. "According to the…"

2. When put in the correct order, the fourth sentence should end with the words   2.____
   A. "…to global climate change."
   B. "…as criteria air pollutants."
   C. "…nitrogen dioxide (NO_2), and sulfur dioxide (SO_2)."
   D. "…health and the environment."

3. If put in the most logical order, the paragraph would end with the words   3.____
   A. "…as criteria air pollutants."
   B. "…to global climate change."
   C. "…benzene, dioxin, and mercury."
   D. "…human health and the environment."

Questions 4-6.

DIRECTIONS: Questions 4 through 6 are to be answered on the basis of the following passage.

Although gentrification has been associated with some positive impacts, such as urban revitalization and lower crime rates, critics charge that it marginalizes racial and ethnic minorities and destroys the character of urban neighborhoods. British sociologist Ruth Glass is credited with coining the term "gentrification" in her 1964 book London: Aspects of Change, which described the transformation that occurred when members of the gentry (an elite or privileged social class) took over working-class districts of London. Gentrification is a type of neighborhood change, a broader term that encompasses various physical, demographic, social, and economic processes that affect distinct residential areas. The arrival of wealthier people leads to new economic development and an increase in property values and rent, which often makes housing unaffordable for longtime residents. Gentrification is a transformation process that typically occurs in urban neighborhoods when higher-income people move in and displace lower-income existing residents.

4. When organized in the correct order, the first sentence of the paragraph should begin with the words
   A. "Gentrification is a type of..."
   B. "British sociologist Ruth..."
   C. "The arrival of..."
   D. "Gentrification is a transformation..."

5. If put together in the correct order, the second to last sentence in the paragraph would end with the words
   A. "...lower-income existing residents."
   B. "...that affect distinct residential areas."
   C. "...character of urban neighborhoods."
   D. "...working-class districts of London."

6. If the author wished to change the beginning of the final sentence to "in the end." to better signal the finish of the paragraph, which of the following words would the phrase appear in front of?
   A. British
   B. Gentrification
   C. Although
   D. The

Questions 7-11.

DIRECTIONS: Questions 7 through 11 are to be answered on the basis of the following passage.

The primary signs of ADHD include a persistent pattern of inattention or hyperactivity lasting in duration for six months or longer with an onset before 12 years of age. Children with ADHD often experience peer rejection, neglect, or teasing and family interactions may contain high levels of discord and negative interactions (APA, 2013). Two primary types of the disorder include inattentive and hyperactive/impulsive, with a combined type when both inattention and hyperactivity occur together. Inattentive ADHD is evidenced by executive functioning deficits such as being off task, lacking sustained focus, and being disorganized. Hyperactive ADHD is evidenced by excessive talkativeness and fidgeting, with an inability to control impulses that may result in harm. Attention Deficit Hyperactivity Disorder (ADHD) is a commonly diagnosed childhood behavioral disorder affecting millions of children in the U.S. every year (National Institute of Mental Health [NIMH], 2012), with prevalence rates between 5% and 11% of the population. Other research has examined singular traits such as executive function deficits in the school setting, task performance in the school setting (Berk, 1986), driving and awareness of time. However, researching academic aspects of the school experience does not provide a comprehensive understanding of the systemic effects of ADHD in the school environment. Historically, much research on ADHD has focused on the academic impact of behavioral symptoms such as reading and mathematics. These behaviors are inappropriate for the child's age level and symptoms typically interfere with functioning in multiple environments.

7. If the author put the paragraph into a logical order, the first sentence would begin with the words
   A. "Inattentive ADHD is…"
   B. "Historically, much research…"
   C. "These behaviors are…"
   D. "Attention Deficit Hyperactivity Disorder…"

8. When put in the correct order, what does the author mean by "These behaviors" in the sentence that begins "These behaviors are…"?
   A. Inattention or hyperactivity
   B. Reading and Mathematics
   C. Peer rejection
   D. Sustained focus

9. If the author wished to split this paragraph into two paragraphs (not necessarily equal parts), the first sentence of the second paragraph would BEGIN with the words
   A. "Historically, much research…"
   B. "Other research has examined…"
   C. "Two primary types of…"
   D. "Inattentive ADHD is evidenced…"

10. When put in the correct order, the third sentence in the paragraph would END with the words
    A. "…an onset before 12 years of age."
    B. "…5% and 11% of the population."
    C. "…such as reading and mathematics."
    D. "…in multiple environments."

11. If the above paragraph was organized correctly, its ending words of the last sentence would be
    A. "…sustained focus, and being disorganized."
    B. "…an onset before 12 years of age."
    C. "…in the school environment."
    D. "…inattention and hyperactivity occur together."

Questions 12-15.

DIRECTIONS: Questions 12 through 15 are to be answered on the basis of the following passage.

Health care fraud imposes huge costs on society. In prosecutions of fraud, the DOJ employs the resources of its own criminal and civil divisions, as well as those of the U.S. Attorneys' Offices, HHS, and the FBI. The FBI estimates that health care fraud accounts for at least three and possibly up to ten percent of total health care expenditures, or somewhere between $82 billion and $272 billion each year. Providers are also careful to screen hires for excluded persons or entities lest they be subject to civil monetary penalties. Several government agencies are involved in fighting health care fraud. Individual states assist the HHS Office of the Inspector General ("OIG") and Centers for Medicare & Medicaid Services ("CMS") to initiate and pursue investigations of Medicare and Medicaid fraud. In addition, the OIG uses its permissive exclusion authority to exclude individuals and entities convicted of health care related crimes from federally funded health care services in order to induce providers to help track fraud through a voluntary disclosure program. $30 to $98 billion dollars of that (approximately 36%) is fraud against the public health programs Medicare and Medicaid. The Department of Justice ("DOJ") and the Department of Health and Human Services ("HHS") enforce federal health care fraud law and regulations.

12. When put together in a logical order, the second sentence of the paragraph would end with the words
    A. "...in fighting health care fraud."
    B. "...$272 billion each year."
    C. "...voluntary disclosure program."
    D. "...to civil monetary penalties."

13. In order to organize the paragraph correctly, the sentence that begins "In addition, the OIG..." should FOLLOW the sentence that begins with the words
    A. "$30 to $98 billion dollars of that..."
    B. "Health care fraud..."
    C. "Individual states assist..."
    D. "In prosecutions of fraud..."

14. The author wishes to split the paragraph into a smaller introductory paragraph followed by a slightly longer body paragraph. Which of the following sentences would be BEST to start the second paragraph?
    A. "$30 to $98 billion dollars of that (approximately 36%) is fraud against the public health care programs Medicare and Medicaid."
    B. "Several government agencies are involved in fighting health care fraud."
    C. "In prosecutions of fraud, the DOJ employs the resources of its own criminal and civil divisions, as well as those of the U.S. Attorneys' Offices, HHS, and the FBI."
    D. "Health care fraud imposes huge costs on society."

15. If put together correctly, the paragraph should end with the words   15._____
    A. "...Attorneys' Offices, HHS, and the FBI."
    B. "...huge costs on society."
    C. "...fighting health care fraud."
    D. "...of Medicare and Medicaid fraud."

Questions 16-19.

DIRECTIONS: Questions 16 through 19 are to be answered on the basis of the following passage.

President Abraham Lincoln advocated for granting amnesty to former Confederates to heal the country after the devastating war. Adams and his fellow Federalist Party members in Congress used the law to jail more than a dozen of his political rivals. In 1977, President Jimmy Carter lifted the restrictions on draft dodgers, granting them unconditional amnesty. The issue of amnesty again arose shortly after the U.S. Civil War (1861-1865). Some U.S. government officials, including Vice President Andrew Johnson, advocating placing severe punishments on the military and civilian leaders of the secessionist Confederate States of America. A century later, the controversial nature of the Vietnam War (1964-1975), combined with the compulsory draft for military service, compelled many young men of eligible age to violate the law to avoid the draft. When Thomas Jefferson, Adams' Vice President and opponent of the Alien and Sedition Acts, won the 1800 presidential election, he declared amnesty for those found to have violated the law. Other young men who were drafted deserted the army and refused to serve. In May 1865, when serving as president following Lincoln's assassination, Johnson issued the Proclamation of Amnesty and Reconstruction, which granted the rights of voting and holding office to most former Confederates. In 1974, President Gerald Ford granted amnesty to deserters and "draft dodgers" on the condition that they swear allegiance to the United States and engage in two years of community service. In 1798, President John Adams signed the Alien and Sedition Acts, a set of four laws that restricted criticism of the federal government.

16. When put in the correct order, the paragraph would begin with the following words.   16._____
    A. "Some U.S. government..."   B. "In May 1865, when..."
    C. "A century later, the..."   D. "In 1798, President..."

17. If put in logical order, what sentence number would the sentence that begins   17._____
    "President Abraham Lincoln..." be?
    A. One   B. Six   C. Five   D. Two

18. The author wants to split this paragraph into three separate paragraphs. The   18._____
    THIRD paragraph should begin with the words
    A. "The issue of amnesty again..."   B. "In 1798, President..."
    C. "In 1977, President Jimmy..."   D. "A century later, the..."

19. When organized in sequential order, the last sentence of the paragraph   19._____
    would end with the words
    A. "...of his political rivals."   B. "...after the devastating war."
    C. "...them unconditional amnesty."   D. "...of the federal government."

Questions 20-22.

DIRECTIONS: Questions 20 through 22 are to be answered on the basis of the following passage.

Throughout history, militias have played an important role in national defense against foreign invaders or oppressors. In the original American colonies, state militias served to keep order and played an important role in the fight for independence from the British during the American Revolutionary War. Since that time, state-level militias have continued to exist in the United States alongside a national standing army, providing additional reserve defense and emergency assistance when needed. Some countries still rely almost entirely on public militias for civil defense. In Switzerland, for example, all able-bodied males must serve as part of the Swiss military or civilian service for several months starting when they turn 20 years old and remain reserve militia for years after. Similarly, in Israel, all non-Arab citizens over the age of 18 are required to serve in the Israel Defense Forces for at least two years; Israel is unique in that it requires military service from female citizens as well as males.

20. When put into the correct order, the paragraph should begin with the words 20.____
    A. "Throughout history, militias…"   B. "Similarly, in Israel…"
    C. "Some countries still rely…"   D. "Since that time, state-level…"

21. The fifth sentence of the paragraph should end with the words 21.____
    A. "…against foreign invaders or oppressors."
    B. "…militias for civil defense."
    C. "…reserve militia for years after."
    D. "…citizens as well as males."

22. The last sentence of the paragraph should end with the words 22.____
    A. "…militias for civil defense."
    B. "…citizens as well as males."
    C. "…against foreign invaders or oppressors."
    D. "…during the American Revolutionary War."

Questions 23-25.

DIRECTIONS: Questions 23 through 25 are to be answered on the basis of the following passage.

Medicines such as herbal and homeopathic remedies differ radically from those typically prescribed by mainstream physicians. These practices derive from different cultural traditions and scientific premises. As of 2012, the Memorial Sloan-Kettering Cancer Center offered hypnosis and tai chi, which is an ancient Chinese exercise, to help eases the pains associated with conventional cancer treatments. Some medical professionals staunchly dismiss a number of alternative techniques and theories as quackery. The concept of alternative medicine encompasses an extremely wide range of therapeutic modalities, from acupuncture to yoga. As of 2012, nearly 40 percent of Americans use some alternative medicines or therapies, according to the National Institutes of Health's National Center for Complementary and Alternative Medicine. Alternative approaches to health, fitness, disease prevention, and treatment are sometimes referred to as holistic health care or natural medicine. These names suggest some of the philosophical foundations shared by traditions such as homeopathy, naturopathy, traditional Chinese medicine and herbal medicine. A University of Pennsylvania study in 2010 found that more than 70 percent of U.S. cancer centers offered information on complementary therapies. Increasingly, health care providers are encouraging patients to combine alternative and conventional (or allopathic) treatments, a practice known as complementary or integrative medicine. In the contemporary United States, the phrase alternative medicine has come to mean virtually any healing or wellness practice not based within the conventional system of medical doctors, nurses, and hospitals. Some of these alternative treatments include acupuncture to alleviate pain and nausea and yoga to help reduce stress and manage pain. Yet taken as a whole, the alternative sector of the health field is enormously popular and rapidly growing. The Health Services Research Journal reported in 2011 that three out of four U.S. health care workers used complementary or alternative medicine practices themselves. Other studies have shown that more medical professionals are recommending that cancer patients seek alternative treatments to deal with the side effects of conventional treatments, such as chemotherapy, radiation, and surgery.

23. When put in the correct order, the first sentence should begin with the words
    A. "A University of Pennsylvania study…"
    B. "Other studies have shown that…"
    C. "Increasingly, health care providers…"
    D. "In the contemporary United States…"

24. If the author were to split the paragraph into two separate ones, the first sentence of the second paragraph should begin with the words
    A. "Alternative approaches to health…"
    B. "The concept of alternative medicine…"
    C. "As of 2012, nearly 40%…"
    D. "These names suggest some…"

25. When put into the correct logical sequence, the paragraph should end with the words
    A. "…Complementary and Alternative Medicine."
    B. "…system of medical doctors, nurses, and hospitals."
    C. "…associated with conventional cancer treatments."
    D. "…health care or natural medicine."

KEY (CORRECT ANSWERS)

1.	A	11.	C
2.	C	12.	B
3.	B	13.	C
4.	D	14.	B
5.	B	15.	A
6.	C	16.	D
7.	D	17.	B
8.	A	18.	D
9.	A	19.	C
10.	D	20.	A

21. C
22. B
23. D
24. A
25. C